11 + NON-VERBAL REASONING WORKBOOK

Contents

Introduction.. 1

Type 1 2

Type 1 Answers.. 11

Type 2 12

Type 2 Answers.. 19

Type 3 20

Type 3 Answers.. 29

Type 4 30

Type 4 Answers.. 46

Type 5 47

Type 5 Answers.. 53

Type 6 54

Type 6 Answers.. 60

Introduction

This Non-Verbal Reasoning (NVR) workbook contains a selection of NVR questions that mimic/mirror the relevant question types and difficulties often seen in the 11plus examinations. This workbook is CEM compatible and contains a comprehensive breakdown of answers on the answer pages.

These questions have been devised by Rachel Higgins BA (Hons). PGCE. MA (ED). Rachel is a qualified teacher who has worked with children of Primary School age for over 25 years, primarily teaching all aspects of the NFER/GL assessment and currently the CEM 11 plus examinations. This book is designed to support and enable children to:

- Recognise patterns and shapes
- Recognise similarities and differences
- Analyse visual information rapidly
- Use analogies
- Predict sequences
- Formulate strategies

As with all 11 plus materials, constant experience in attempting a variety of question types is invaluable and this workbook plays an integral part of a child's 11 plus study programme.

11 Plus **Reasoning Scheme**

The **Reasoning Scheme** is a kinaesthetic approach to Non-Verbal Reasoning which has been developed by Rachel Higgins alongside Becky Newman. This approach uses tried and tested materials that facilitates analysis of the visual information in NVR questions and encourages the use of these techniques to answer questions quickly, accurately and with ease. The **Reasoning Scheme** is used in all 11 plus pass lessons.

Please see: **www.11pluspass.co.uk**

Type 1

If image 1 relates to image 2, what does image 3 relate to?

Question 1.1

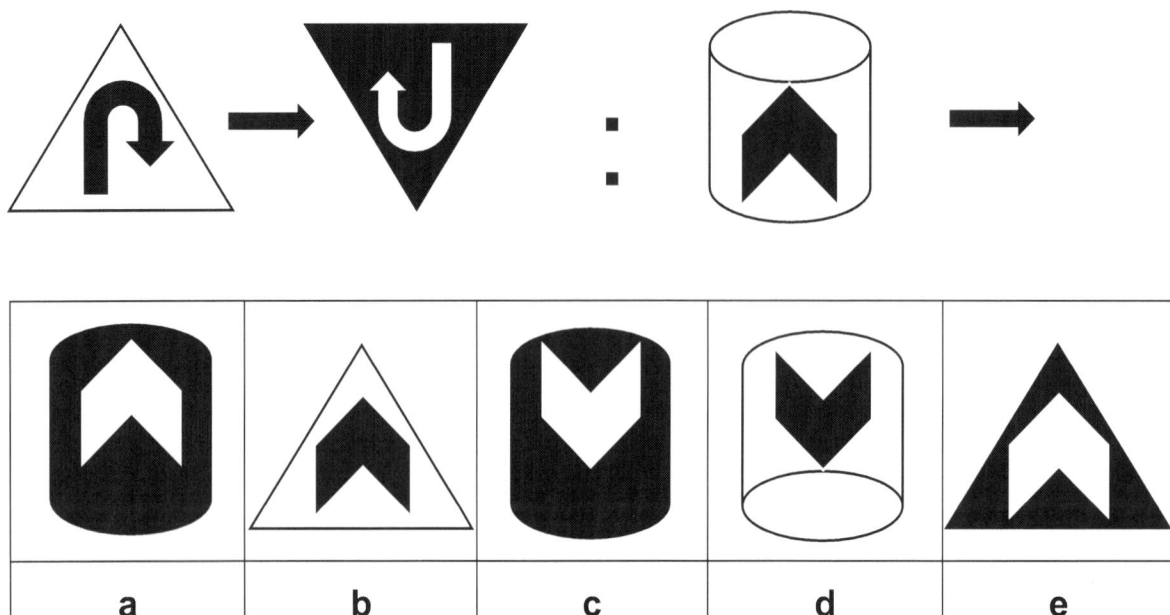

Question 1.2

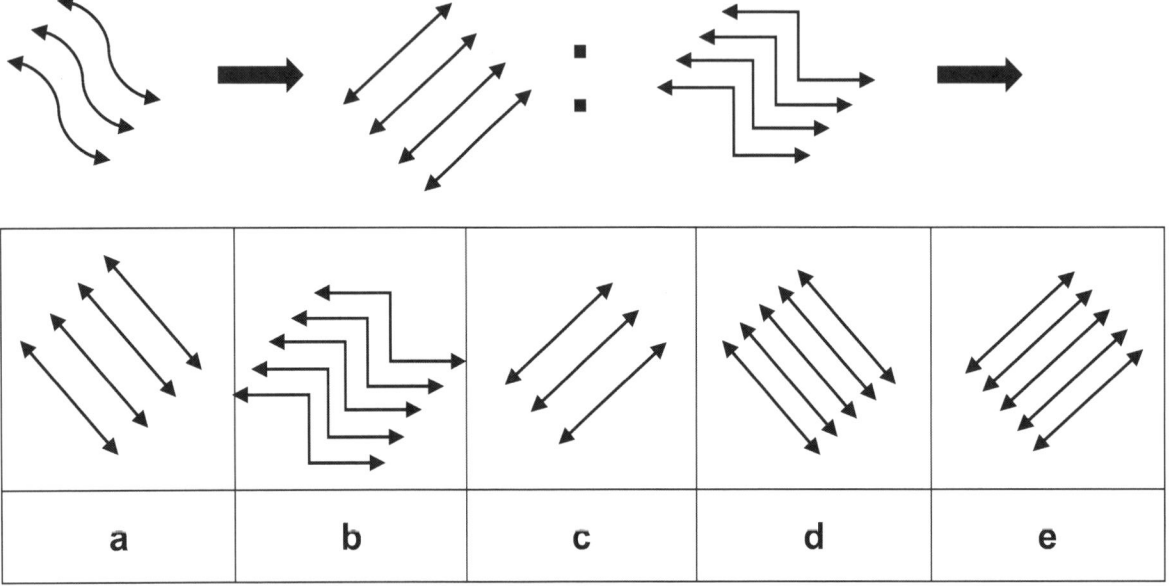

Question 1.3

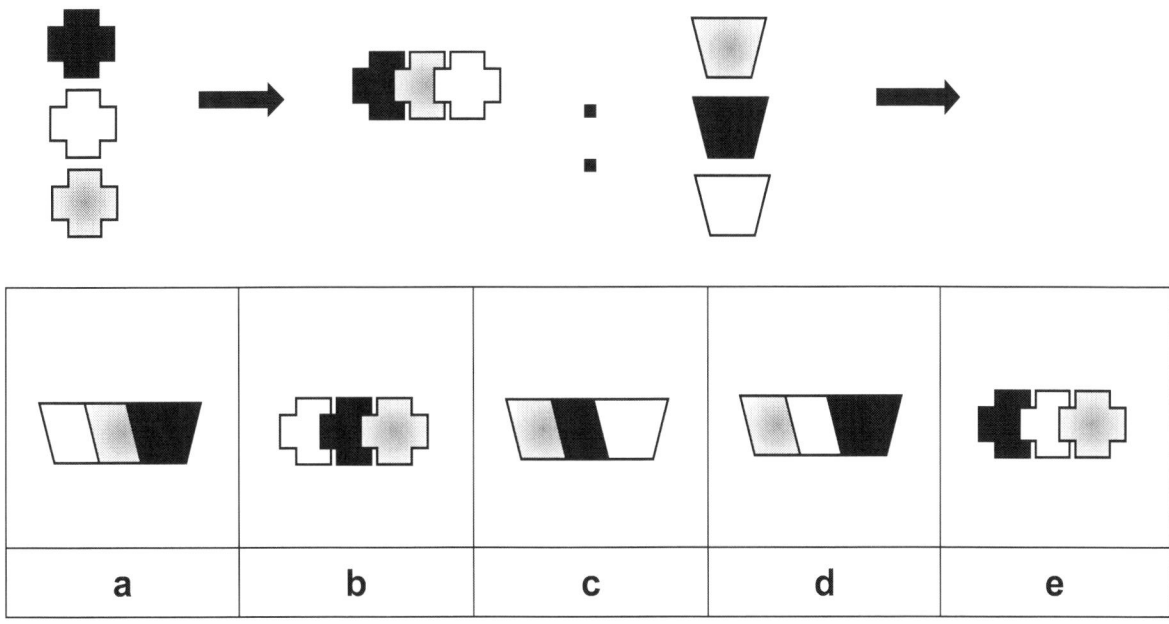

Question 1.4

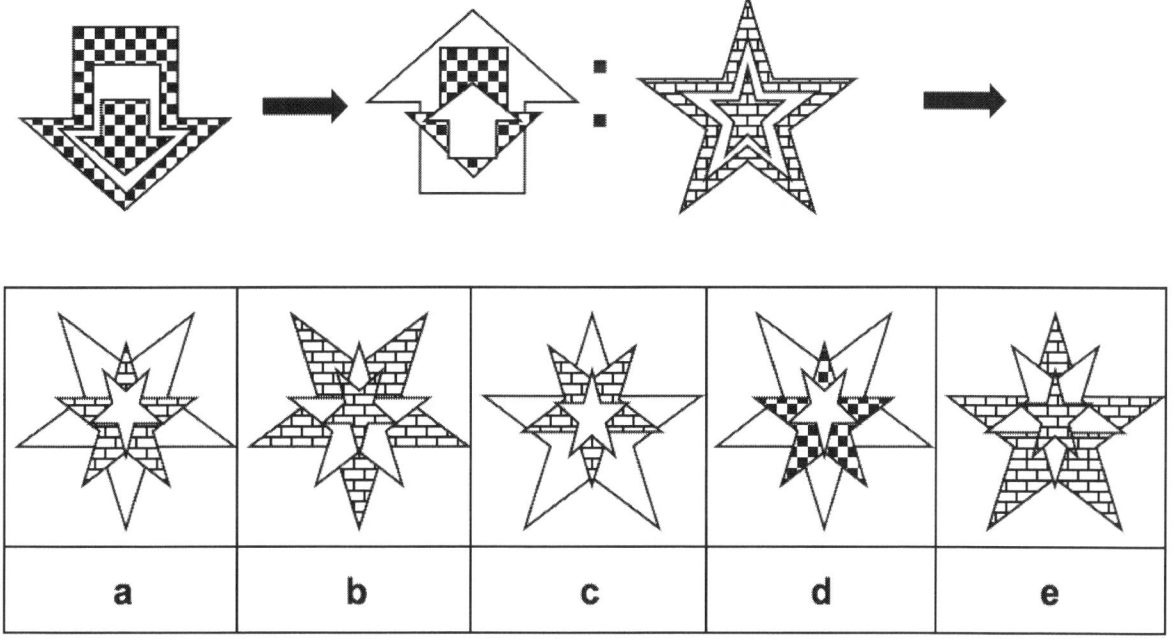

Question 1.5

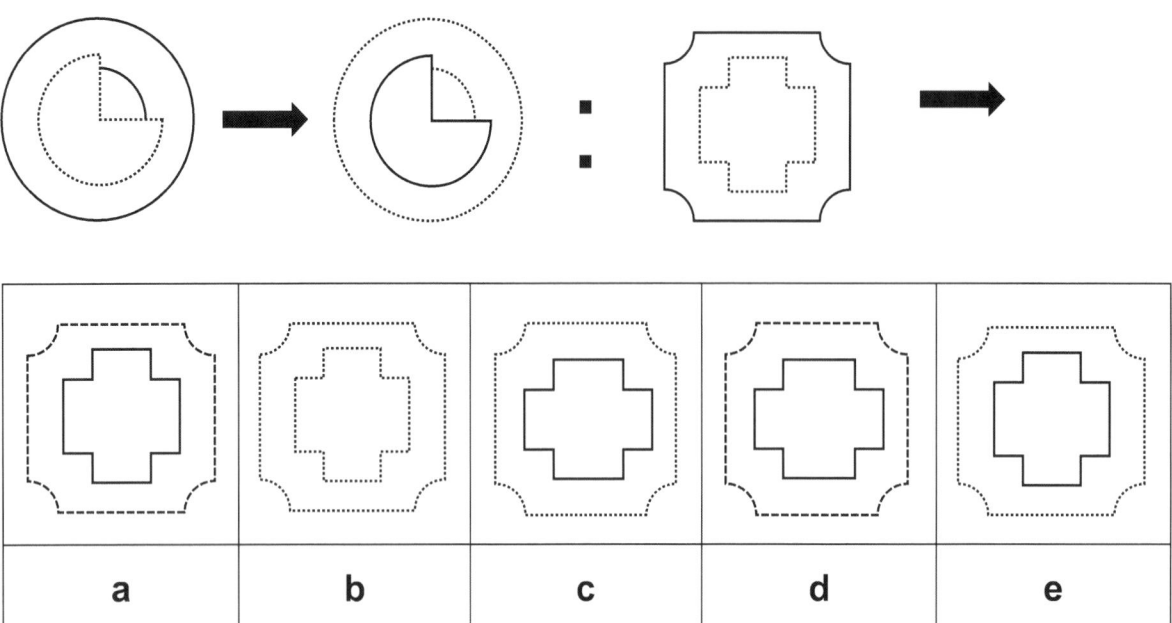

Question 1.6

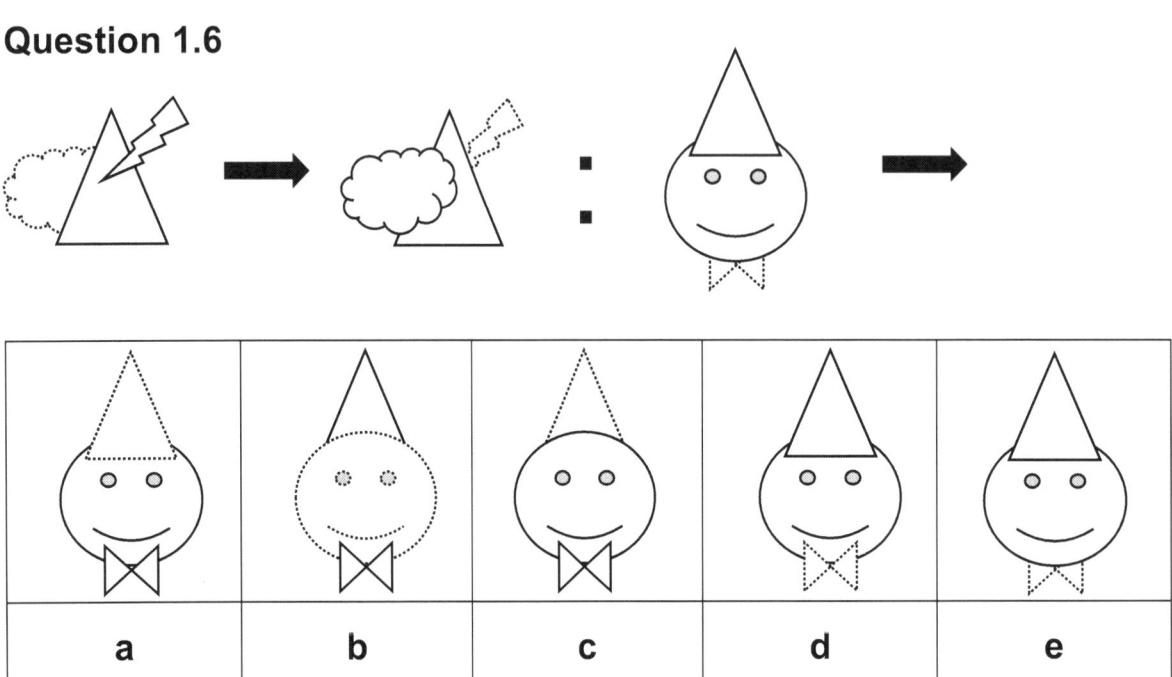

Question 1.7

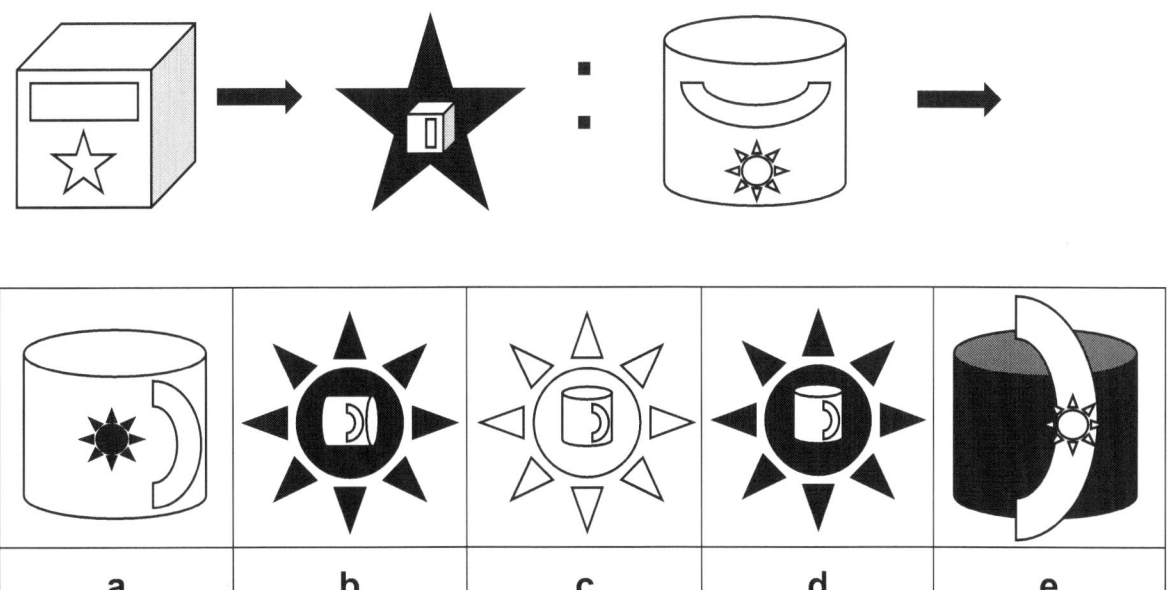

Question 1.8

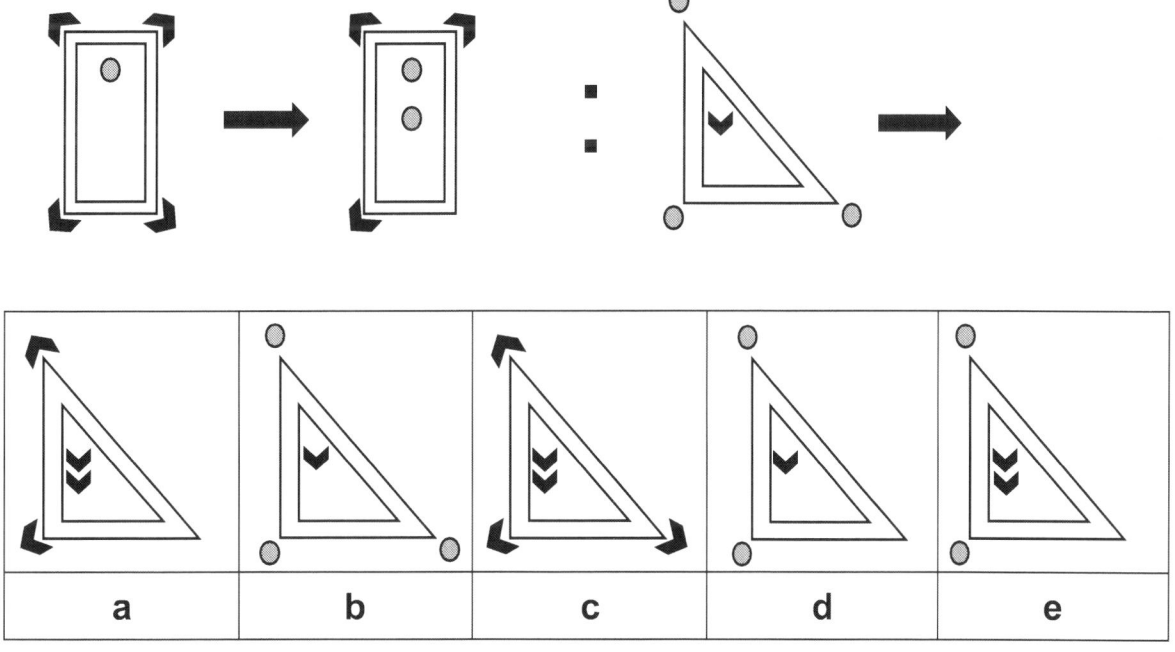

Question 1.9

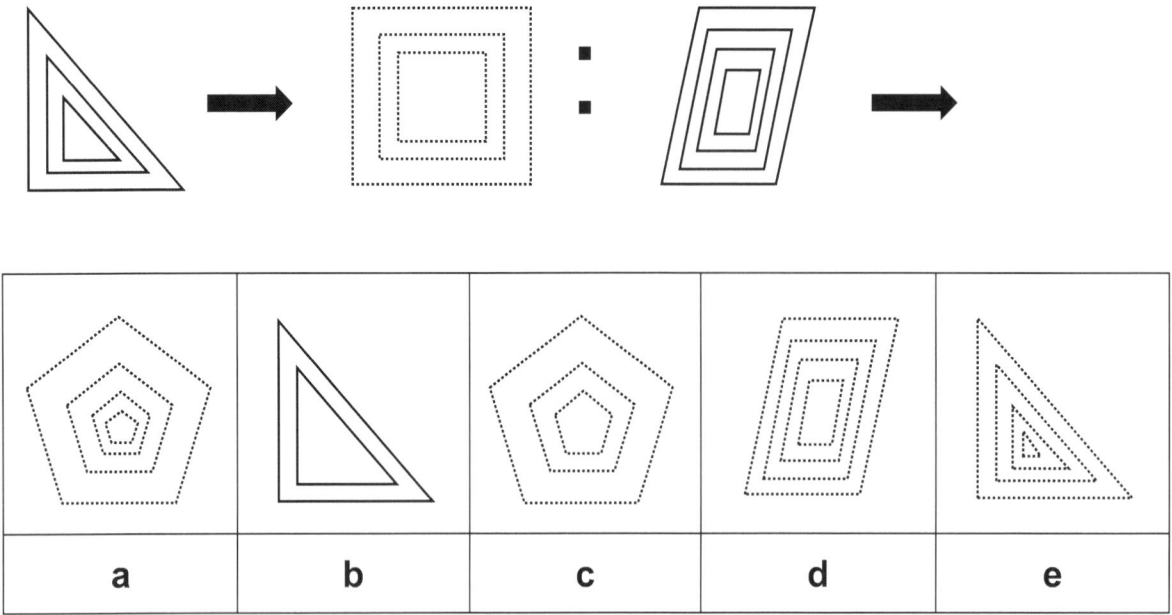

Question 1.10

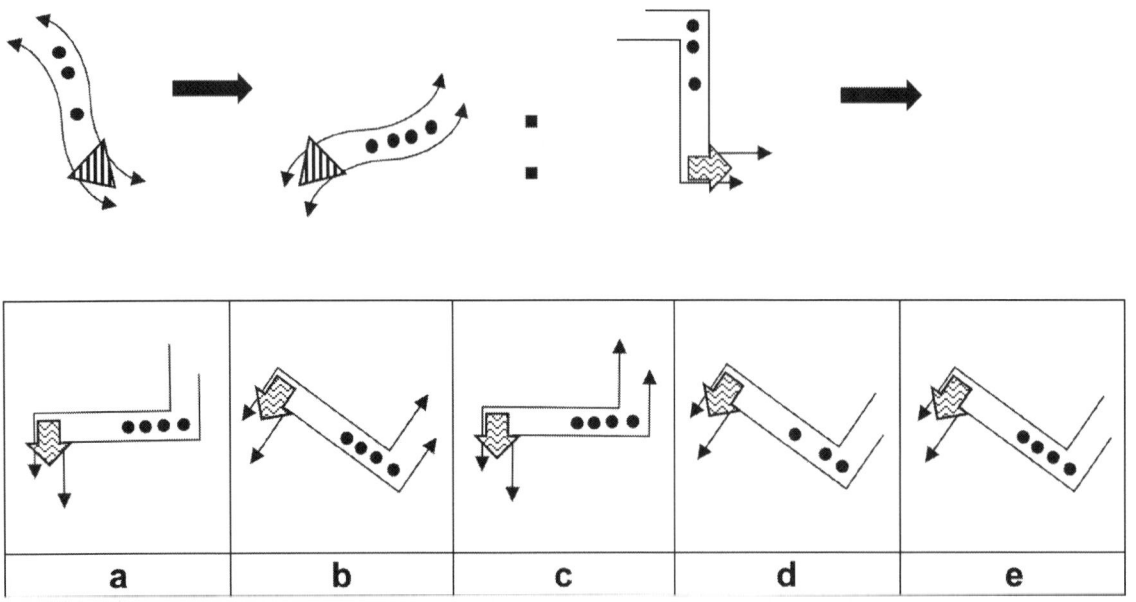

Question 1.11

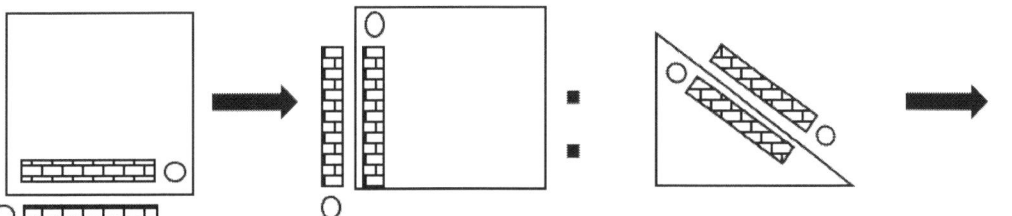

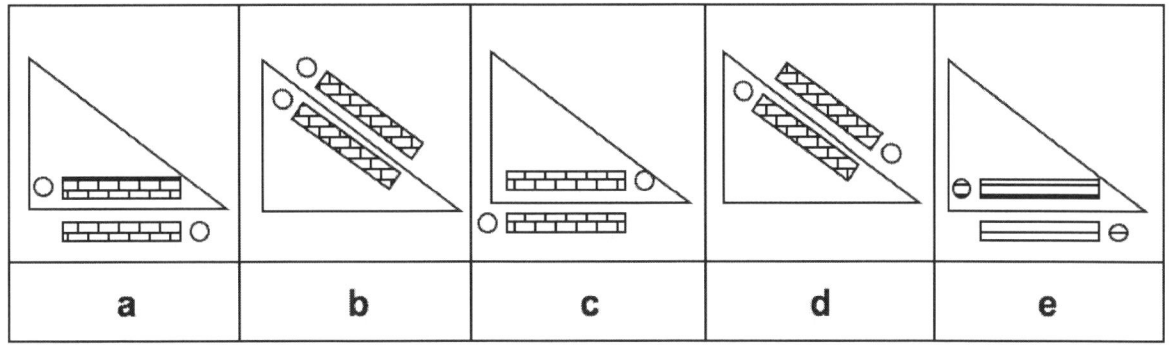

Question 1.12

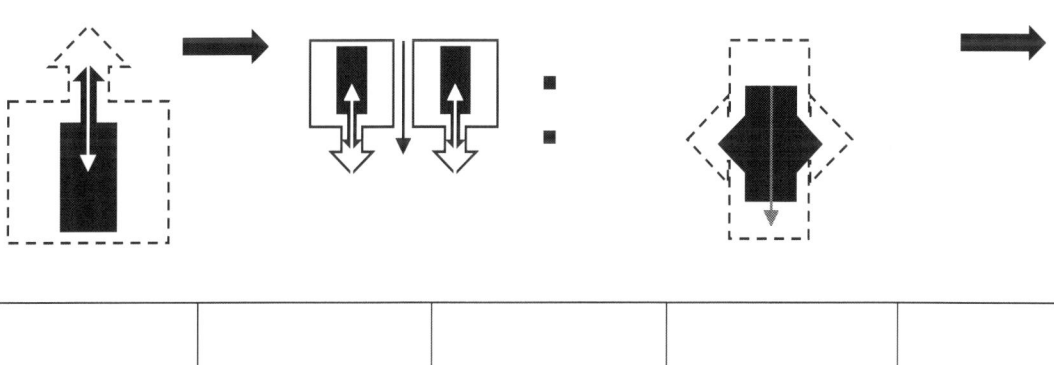

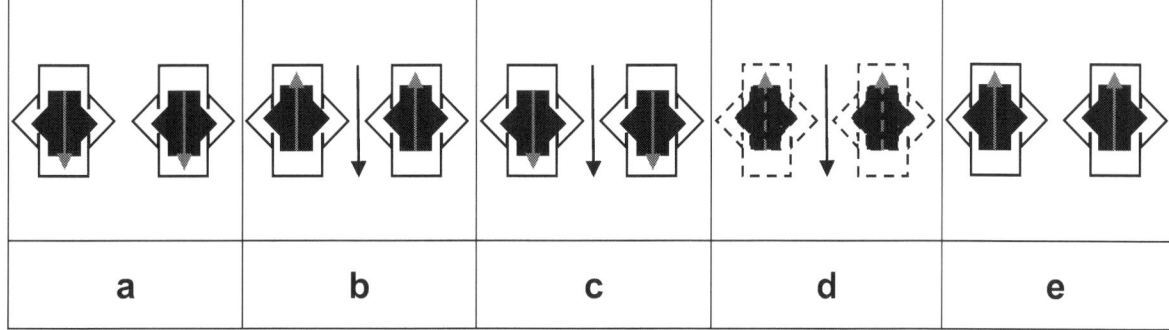

Question 1.13

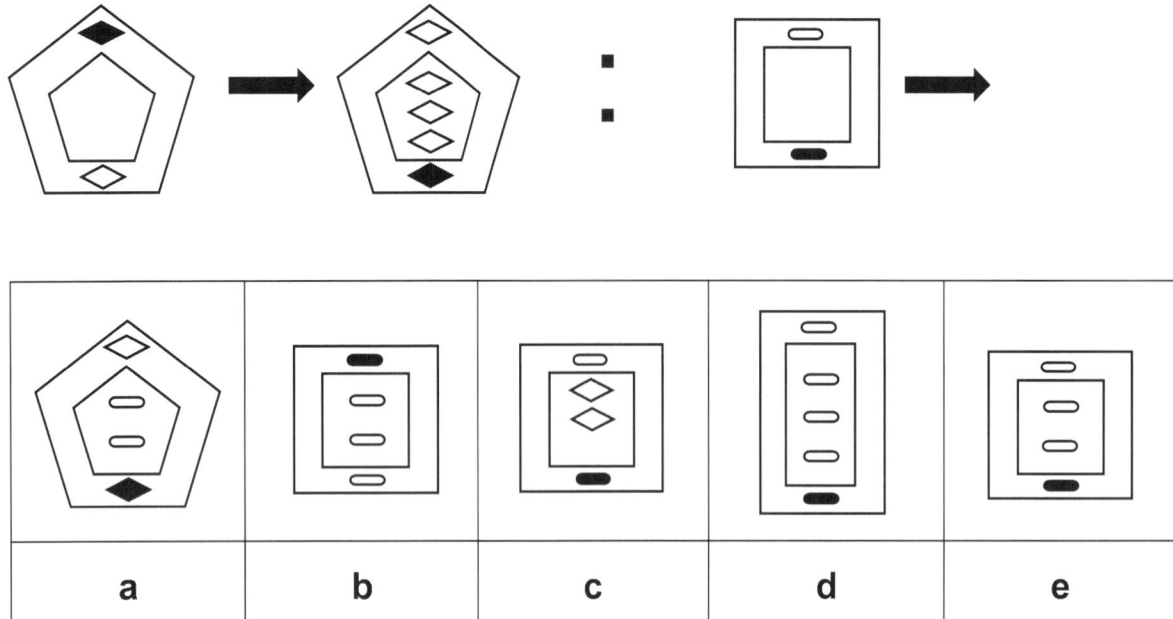

a	b	c	d	e

Question 1.14

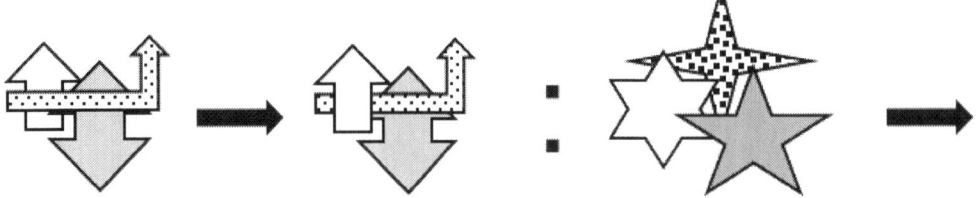

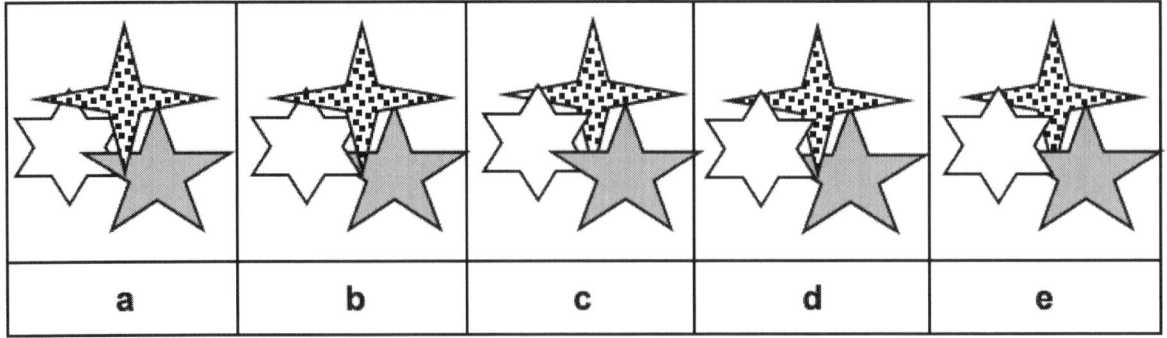

a	b	c	d	e

Question 1.15

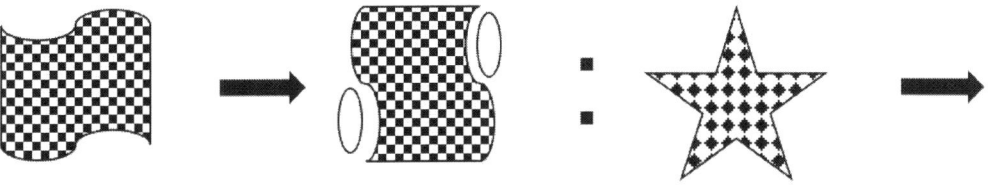

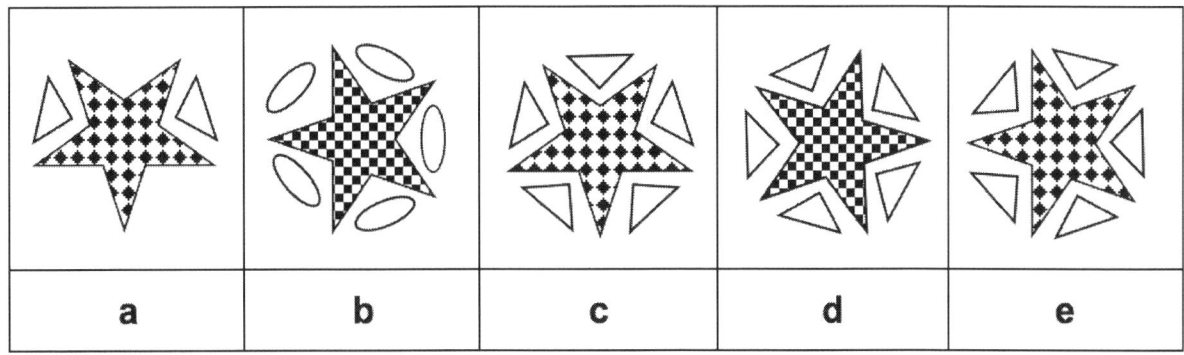

Question 1.16

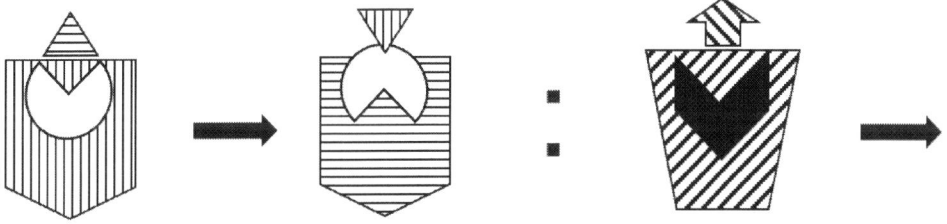

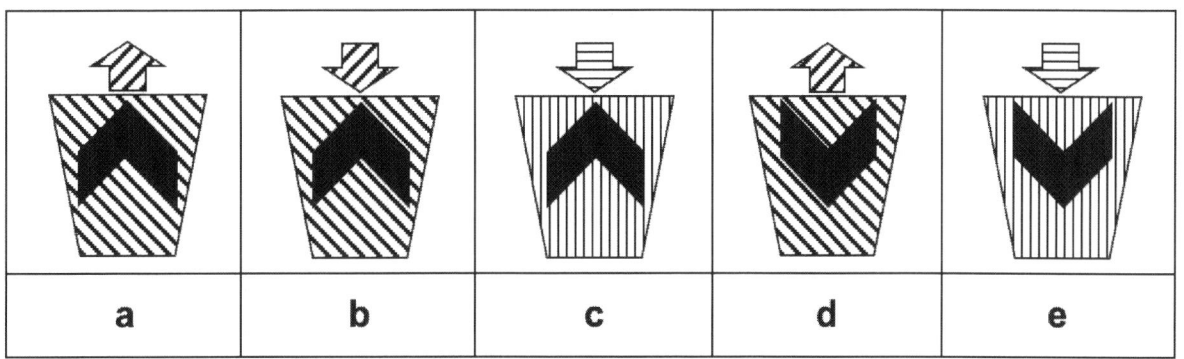

Question 1.17

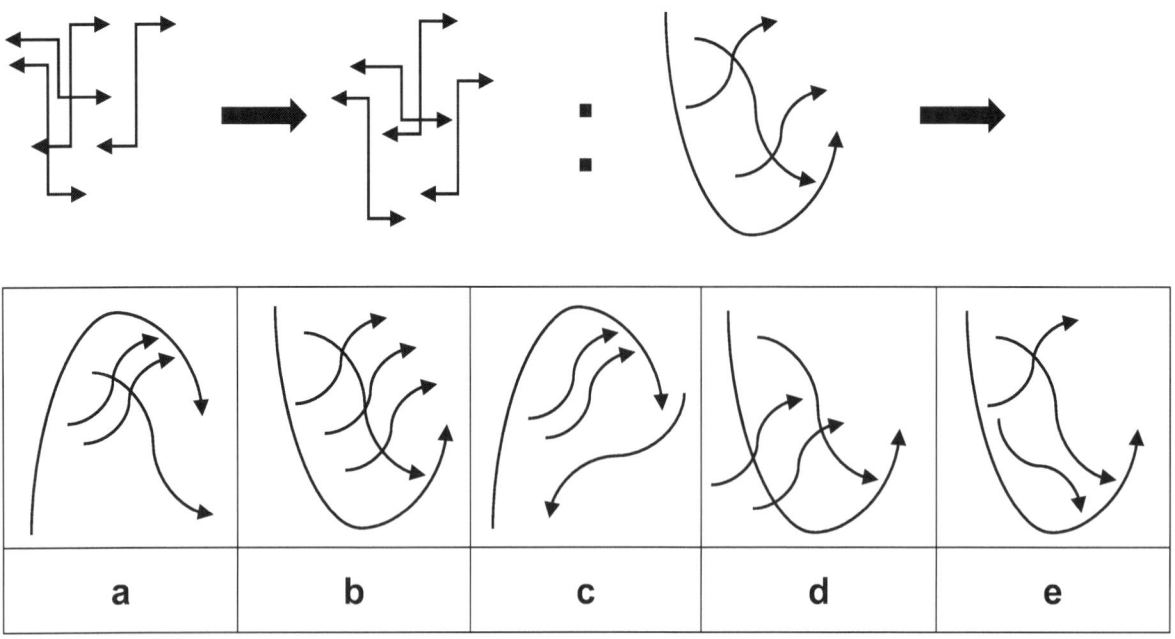

Question 1.18

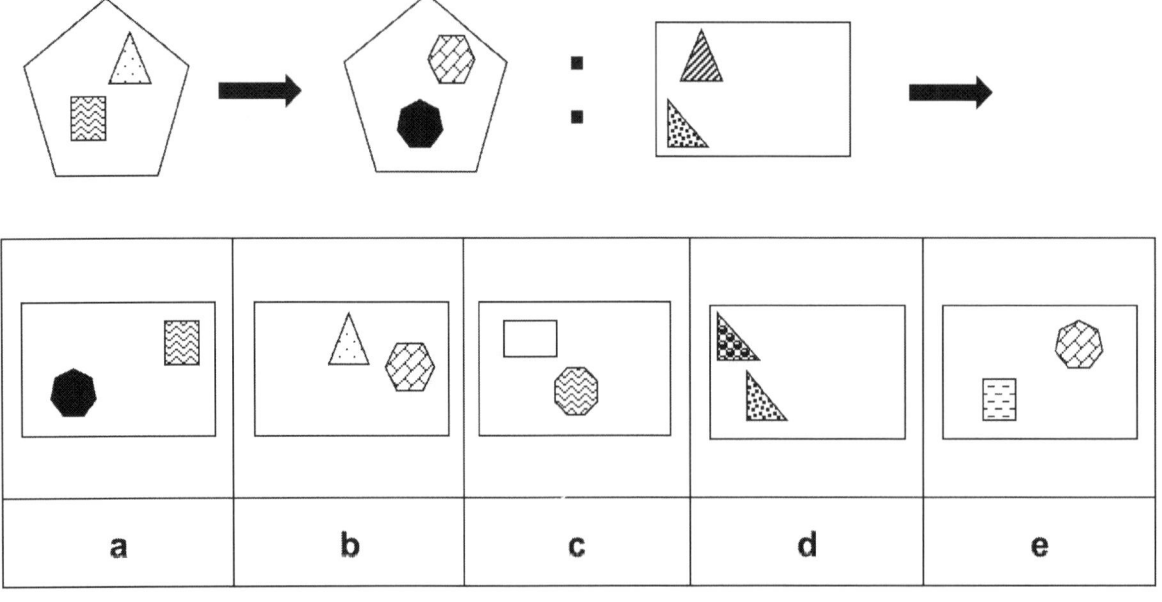

Type 1 Answers

1.1	C	Main shape is rotated. Middle shaped is rotated. Colours are reversed.
1.2	E	Lines have increased by one. Lines straighten. Lines point to the right
1.3	D	All shapes are layered. Top shape becomes the shape on the left. Middle shape becomes the shape on the right. Bottom shape becomes the shape in the middle.
1.4	A	Outside shape is rotated. Centre shape is rotated. Middle shape remains in position. Patterns are reversed.
1.5	E	Outline of all shapes change from broken lines to solid or reverse.
1.6	C	Centre shape remains unchanged. Shapes layered either move forward to backwards and change their lines from solid to broken or reverse.
1.7	D	Small shape at the bottom centre becomes the outside main shape and changes colour. Large shape shrinks. The top small shape and becomes rotated inside.
1.8	E	Outside shapes on vertices reduce in number by one. Reducing from the bottom right. Inside small shapes increase by one.
1.9	A	Shapes are grouped in threes. The outline changes from a solid line to a broken one. The amount of vertices of the shapes increase by one.
1.10	A	The amount of circles inside the shapes increase by one. The arrows on the line terminals remain the same. Image rotated right by 90 degrees
1.11	A	Pattern fill remains the same. Main shape remains the same. Rectangles shift to the next line clockwise. Circles are opposite ends to each other.
1.12	B	Main image as whole shrinks and duplicates. Broken line changes to solid line. Arrow appear in between duplicates and points down.
1.13	B	Outside shape remains the same. The small identical shapes swap colour.
1.14	A	Three shapes are layered. The bottom shape moves in front all shapes. The top shape sandwiches between the other two shapes.
1.15	E	The ovals follow the curve of the large shape. Triangles follow the ident of the star. The large shape rotates to the left by 90 degrees
1.16	B	The fill in the large and small shape outside changes the direction of its stripe. The medium and small outside shapes inverts. The lines rotate by 90 degrees
1.17	E	The amount of crossing arrows decreases by one.
1.18	C	The amount of total vertices of the smaller shapes increase by six.

Type 2

The two letters are a code. What is the code for the last image?

Question 2.1

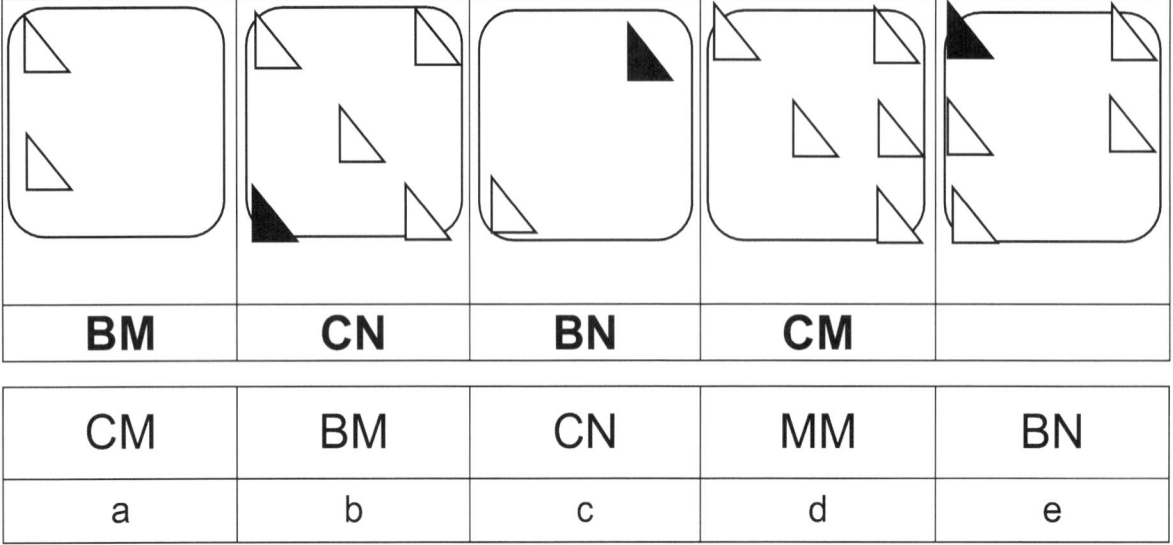

BM	CN	BN	CM	

CM	BM	CN	MM	BN
a	b	c	d	e

Question 2.2

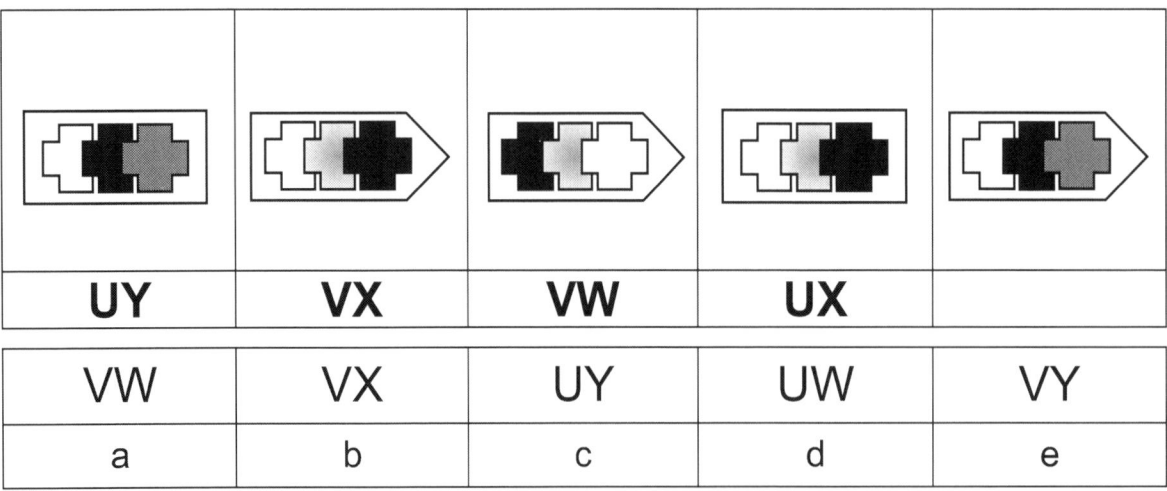

UY	VX	VW	UX	

VW	VX	UY	UW	VY
a	b	c	d	e

Question 2.3

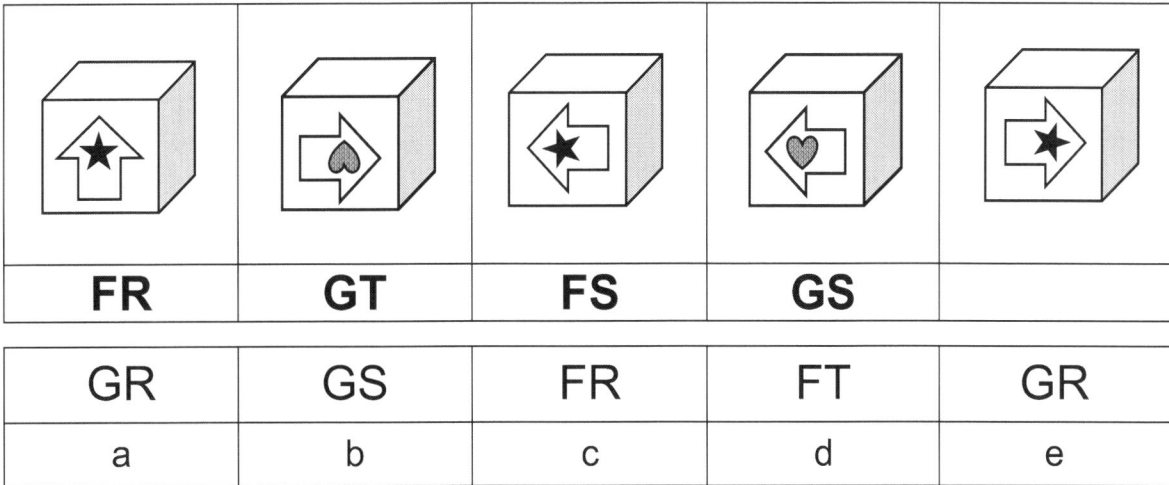

FR	GT	FS	GS	
GR	GS	FR	FT	GR
a	b	c	d	e

Question 2.4

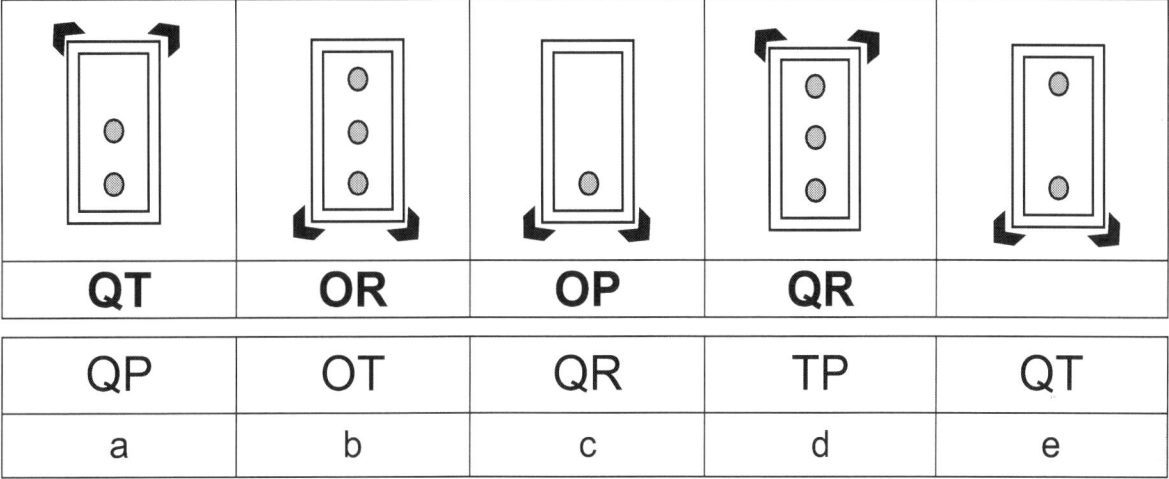

QT	OR	OP	QR	
QP	OT	QR	TP	QT
a	b	c	d	e

Question 2.5

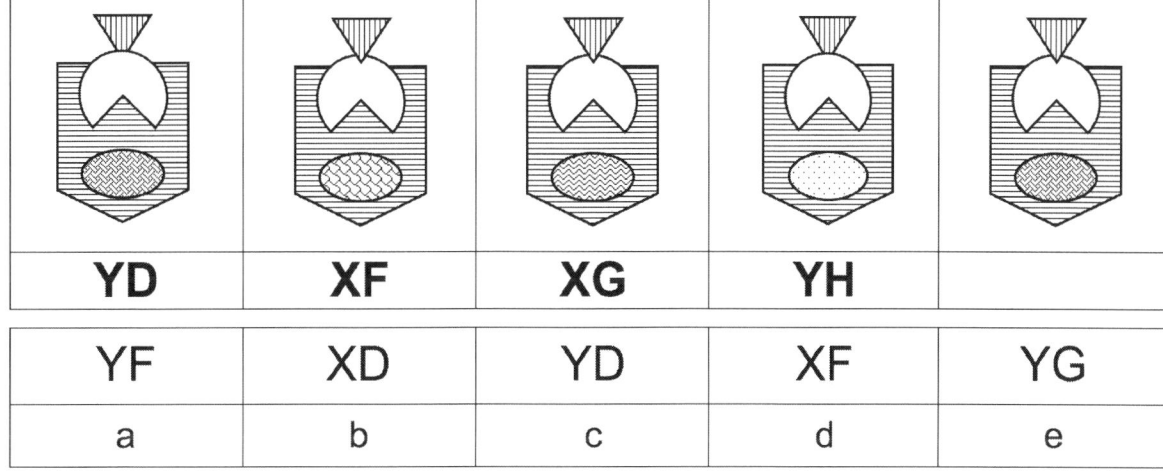

YD	XF	XG	YH	
YF	XD	YD	XF	YG
a	b	c	d	e

Question 2.6

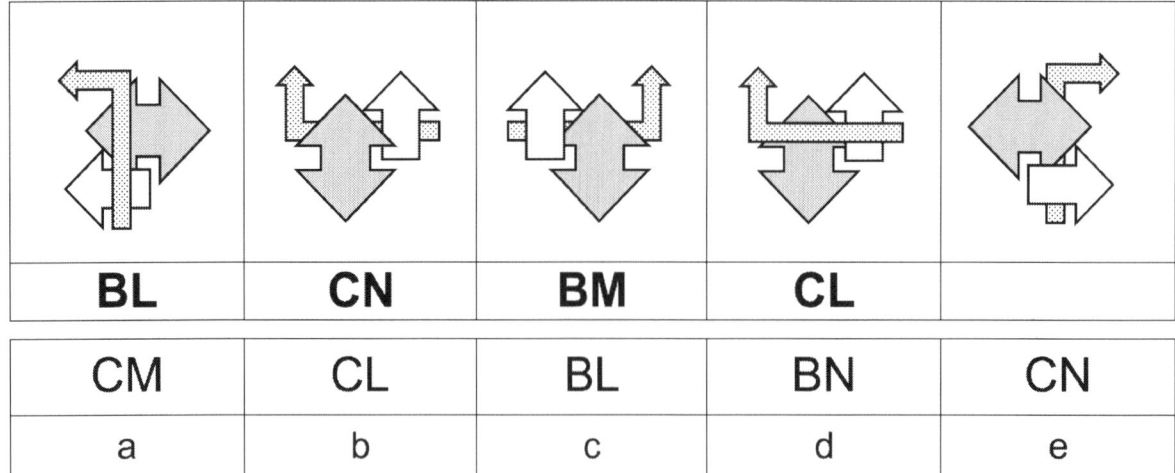

BL	**CN**	**BM**	**CL**	
CM	CL	BL	BN	CN
a	b	c	d	e

Question 2.7

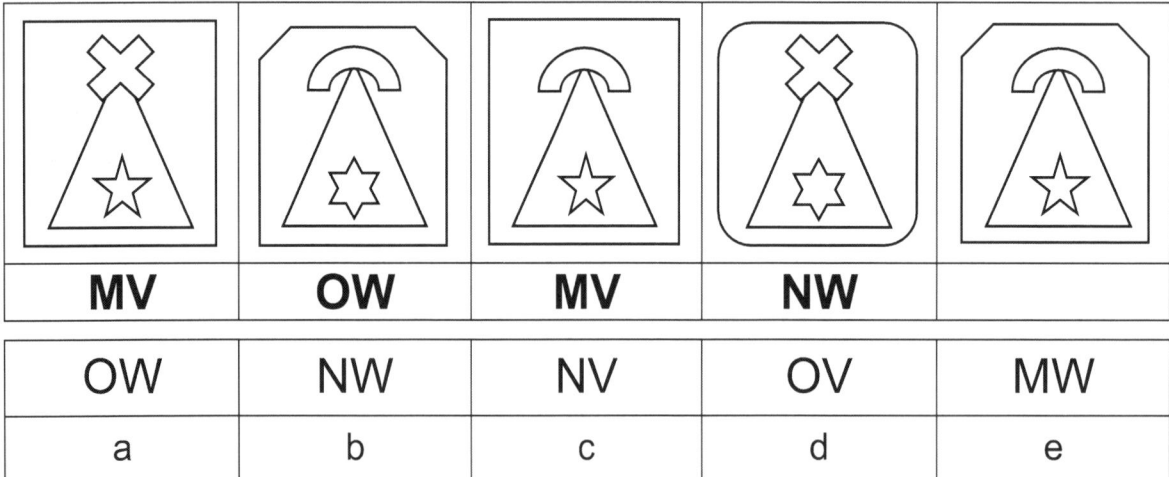

MV	**OW**	**MV**	**NW**	
OW	NW	NV	OV	MW
a	b	c	d	e

Question 2.8

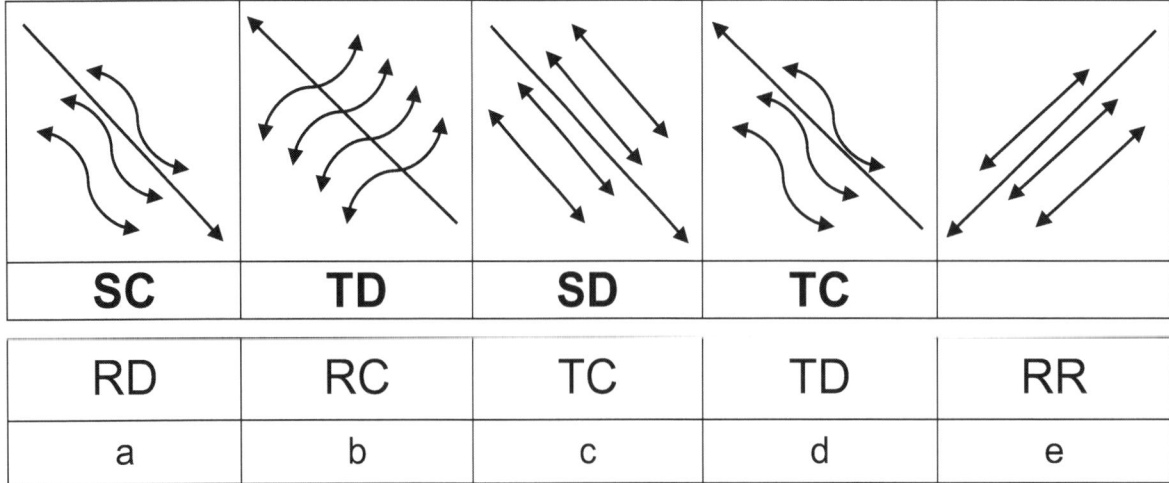

SC	**TD**	**SD**	**TC**	
RD	RC	TC	TD	RR
a	b	c	d	e

Question 2.9

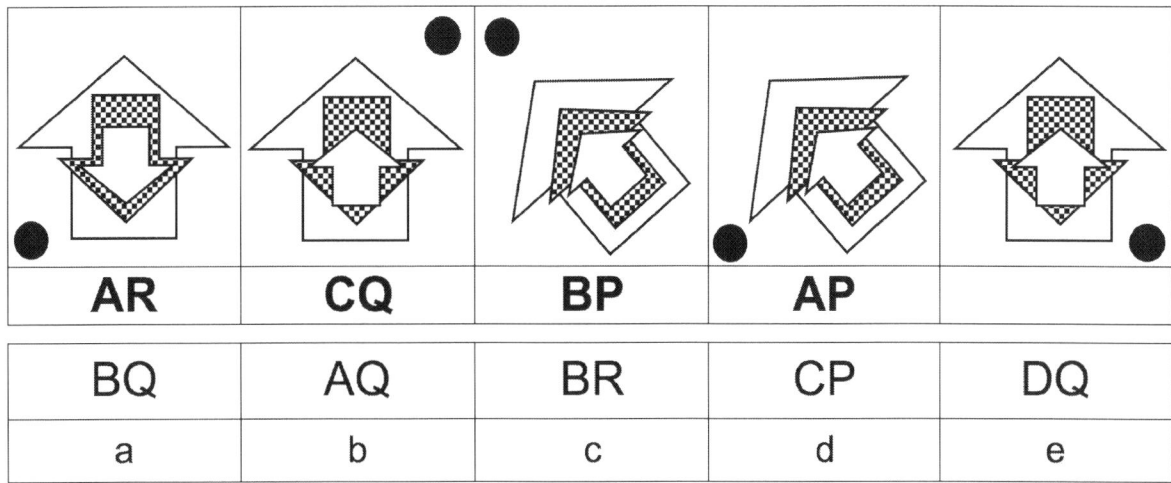

BQ	AQ	BR	CP	DQ
a	b	c	d	e

Question 2.10

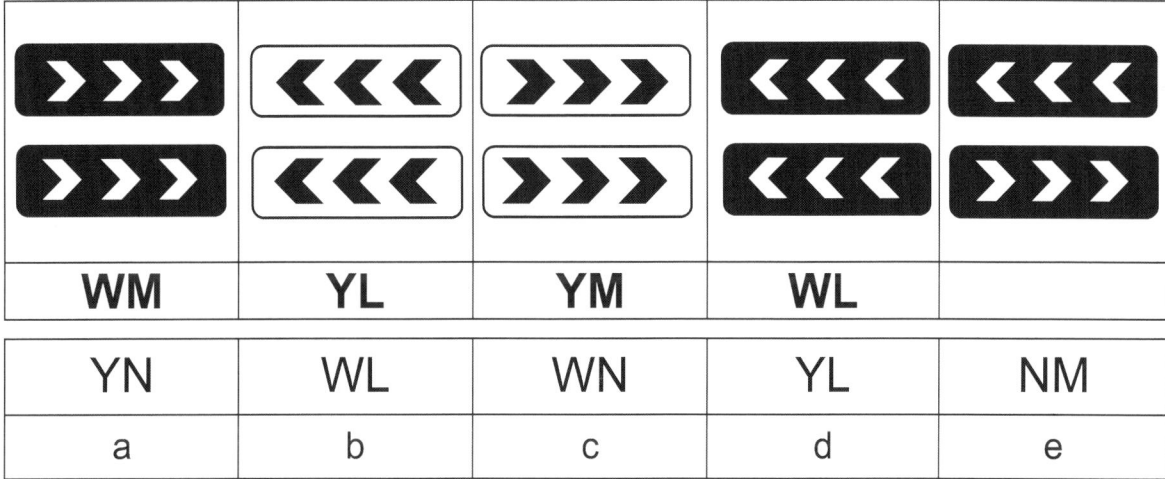

YN	WL	WN	YL	NM
a	b	c	d	e

Question 2.11

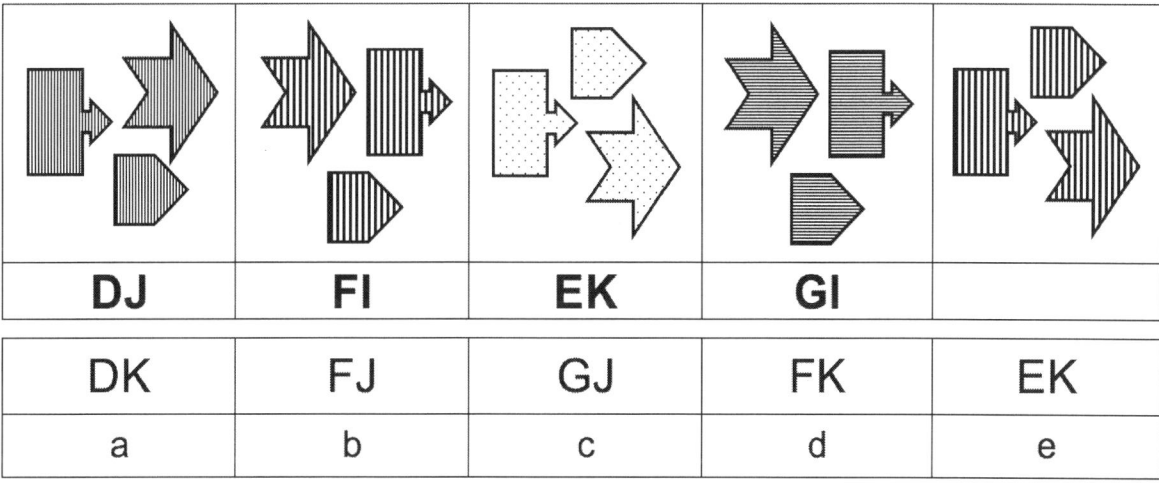

DK	FJ	GJ	FK	EK
a	b	c	d	e

Question 2.12

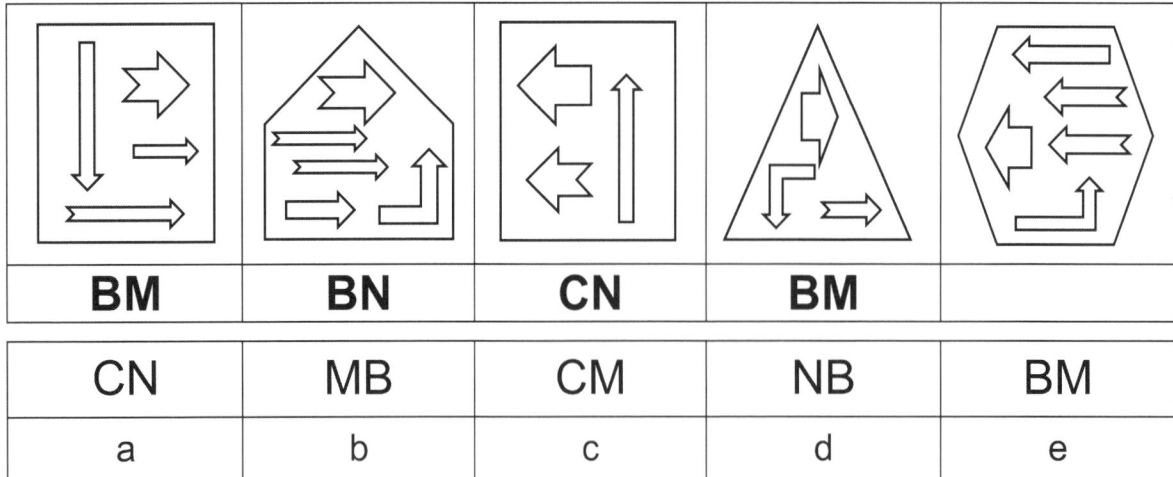

CN	MB	CM	NB	BM
a	b	c	d	e

Question 2.13

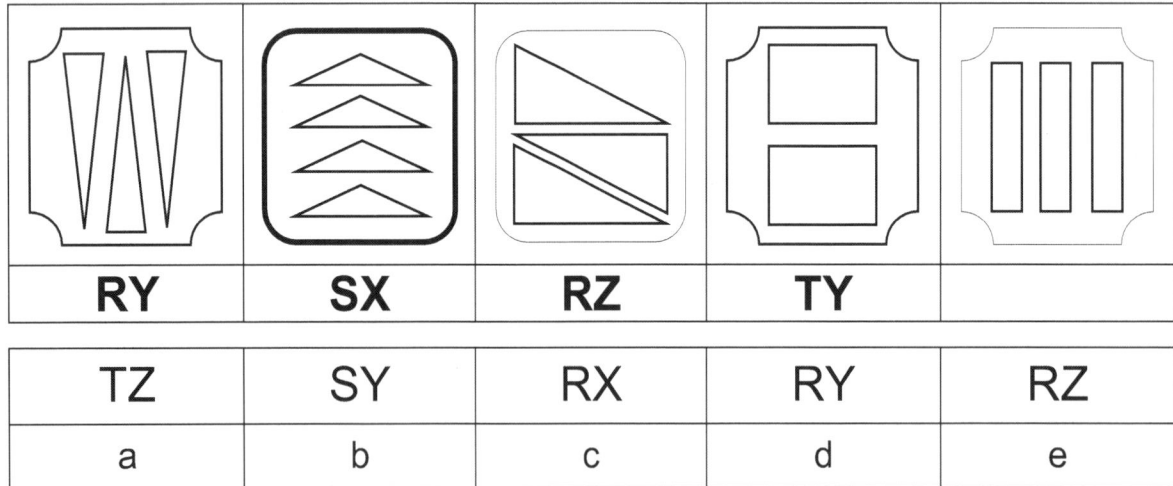

TZ	SY	RX	RY	RZ
a	b	c	d	e

Question 2.14

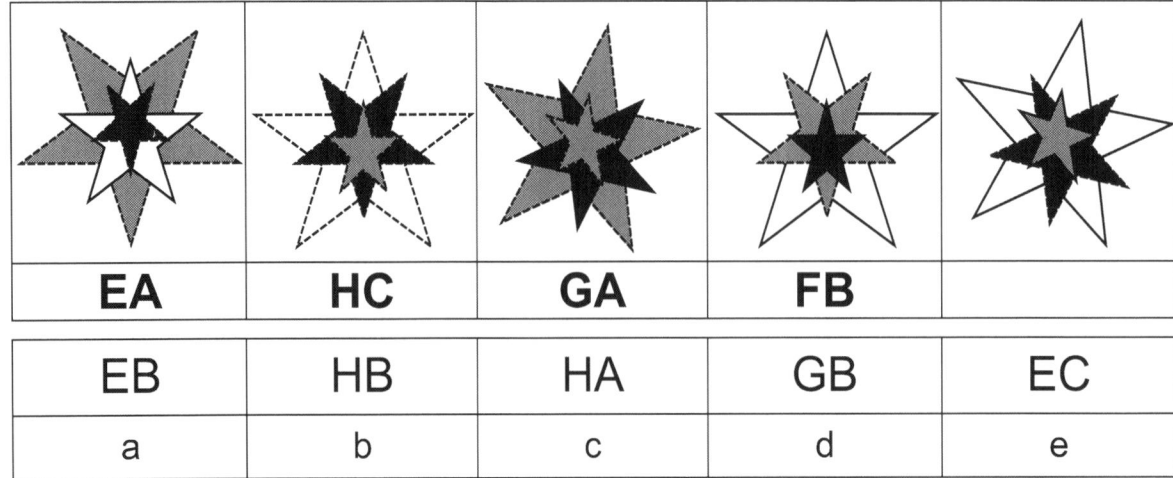

EB	HB	HA	GB	EC
a	b	c	d	e

Question 2.15

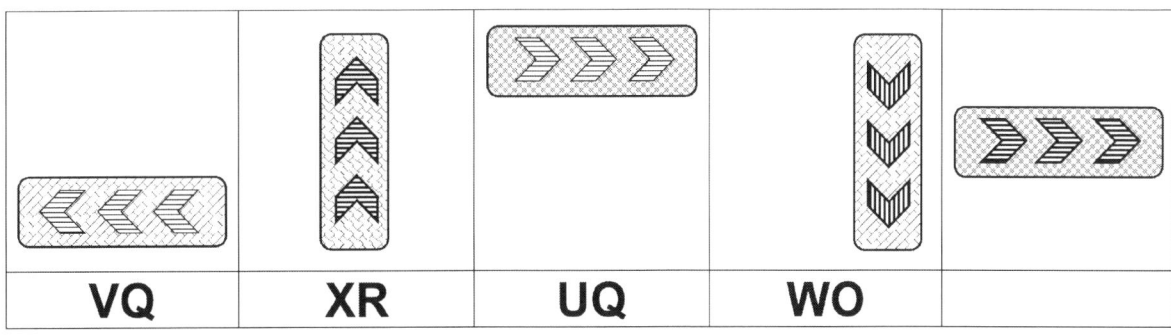

VQ	XR	UQ	WO	
UR	UQ	YQ	WR	YR
a	b	c	d	e

Question 2.16

JO	MP	KO	LN	
LO	MN	LP	MO	KO
a	b	c	d	e

Question 2.17

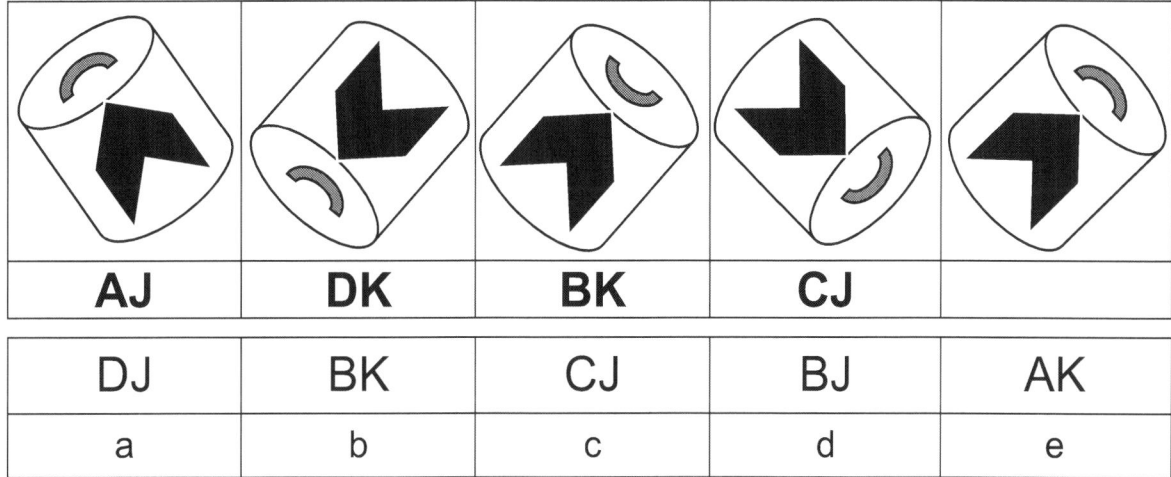

AJ	DK	BK	CJ	
DJ	BK	CJ	BJ	AK
a	b	c	d	e

Question 2.18

YN	XM	WM	YZ	
XN	WN	YZ	WM	WZ
a	b	c	d	e

Type 2 Answers

2.1	**C**	C=Five Triangles B=Two Triangles M=All white N=One black
2.2	**E**	U=Rectangle V=Arrow shape X=Coloured shapes in order: White, Grey and Black Y= Coloured shapes in order: White, Black and Grey W= Coloured shapes in order: Black, Grey and White
2.3	**D**	F=Black Star G=Spotted Heart S=Arrow points to the left R= Arrow points upward T= Arrow points to the right
2.4	**B**	O=two shapes on bottom vertices Q= two shapes on top vertices P=one spot R=three spots T=two spots
2.5	**B**	X=triangle in front Y= triangle behind D=Spotted rectangle fill F=Scale fill G=Wavy line fill H=Spotted fill
2.6	**A**	B / C= Rotations of same grouping of shapes L=Spotted arrow at front M=White arrow at front N=Grey arrow at front
2.7	**D**	M=Rectangle around whole image N=Curved rectangle around whole image O= Rectangle with two corner cut off around whole image V= Five-point star W=Six-point star
2.8	**B**	S=Arrow from top left corner points down T= Arrow from top left corner points up R= Arrow from top right corner points down C=Three smaller arrows D= Four smaller arrows
2.9	**E**	A=Circle in bottom left B= Circle in top left C= Circle in top right D= Circle in bottom right R= Small white arrow points down P= Small white arrow points to top left Q= Small white arrow points up
2.10	**C**	Y= Black arrows W=White arrows L=Arrows point to the left M= Arrows point to the right N= Arrows point both ways
2.11	**D**	D= Thin vertical fill E= Wide vertical fill F=Thick line vertical fill G=Black fill I / J / K =Three shapes in same position
2.12	**A**	B=The amount of arrows matches the amount of vertices in surrounding shape C= The amount of arrows doesn't match the amount of vertices in surrounding shape N= One arrow points up M=One arrow points down
2.13	**E**	R=Three smaller shapes S= Four smaller shapes T= Two smaller shapes X=Thick outline on large shape Y= Medium outline on large shape Z= Fine outline on large shape
2.14	**B**	E=Black, White, Grey F=Black, Grey, White G=Grey, Black, Grey H=Grey, Black, White A= One star has solid lines B= Two stars have solid lines C= No stars have solid lines
2.15	**E**	U= Rectangle at top V= Rectangle at bottom X= Rectangle in middle vertically W= Rectangle at right Y= Rectangle at middle horizontally Q=Thin horizontal stripes R= Thick horizontal stripes O= Thick vertical stripes
2.16	**D**	J= Stripes from bottom left to top right K= Stripes from bottom right to top left L= Horizontal stripes M= Vertical stripes N= One star and cross on top O=Two stars and cross on top P= Three stars on top
2.17	**D**	A= Black arrow points to top left B= Black arrow points to top right C= Black arrow points to bottom right D= Black arrow points to bottom left J= Black arrow points to inside curve of small shape K=Black arrow points to outside curve of small shape
2.18	**B**	W=thin line on top X= thin line on left Y= thin line on bottom M= Seven-point star N= Eight-point star Z= Ten-point star

Type 3

Each question shows a sequence. What is the missing image?

Question 3.1

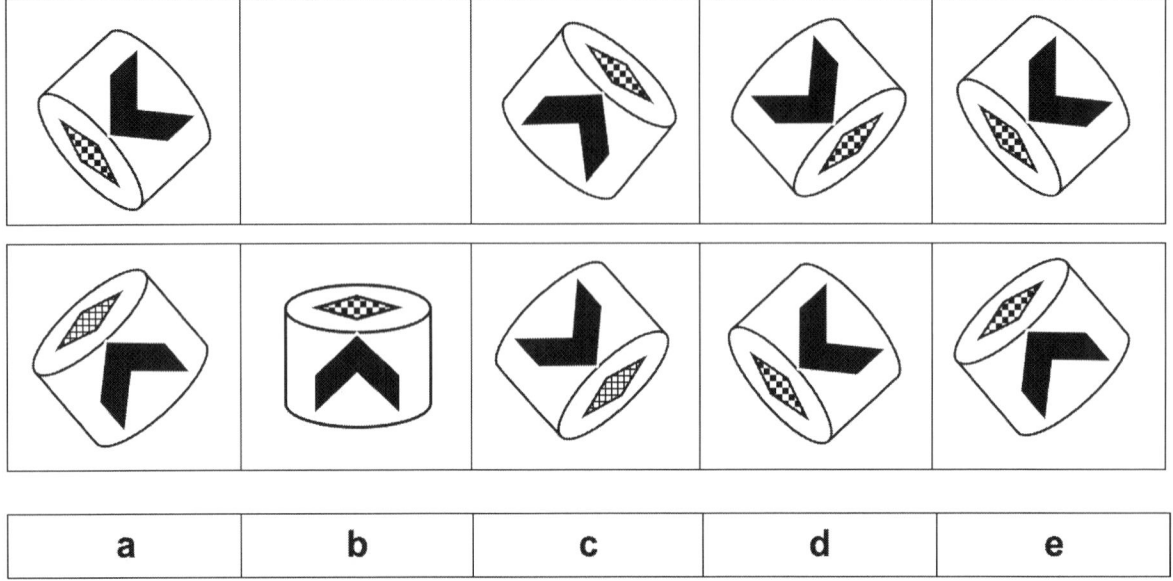

Question 3.2

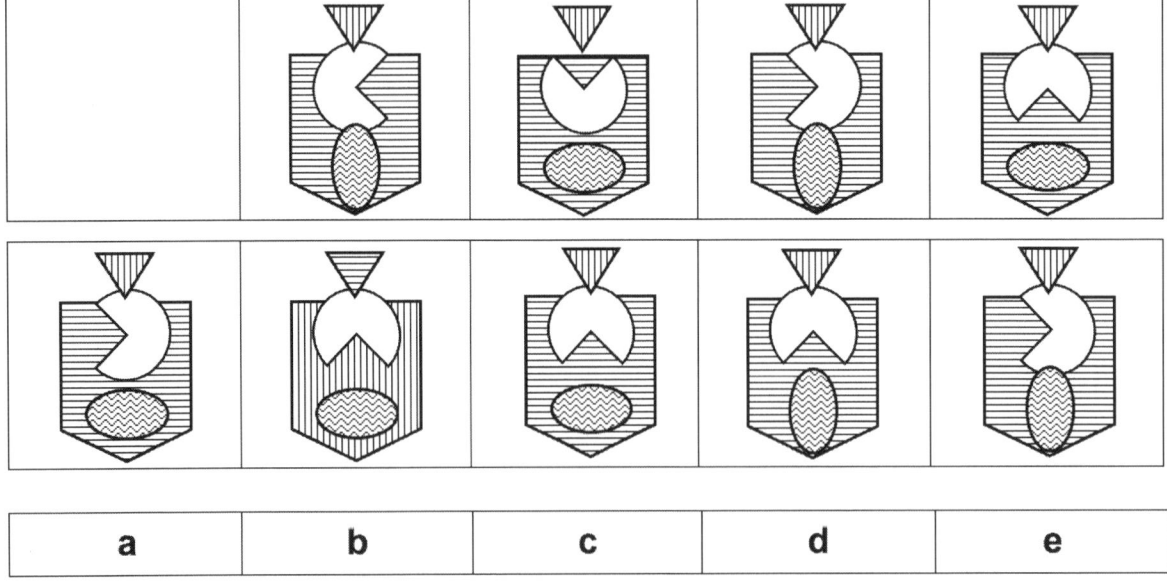

Question 3.3

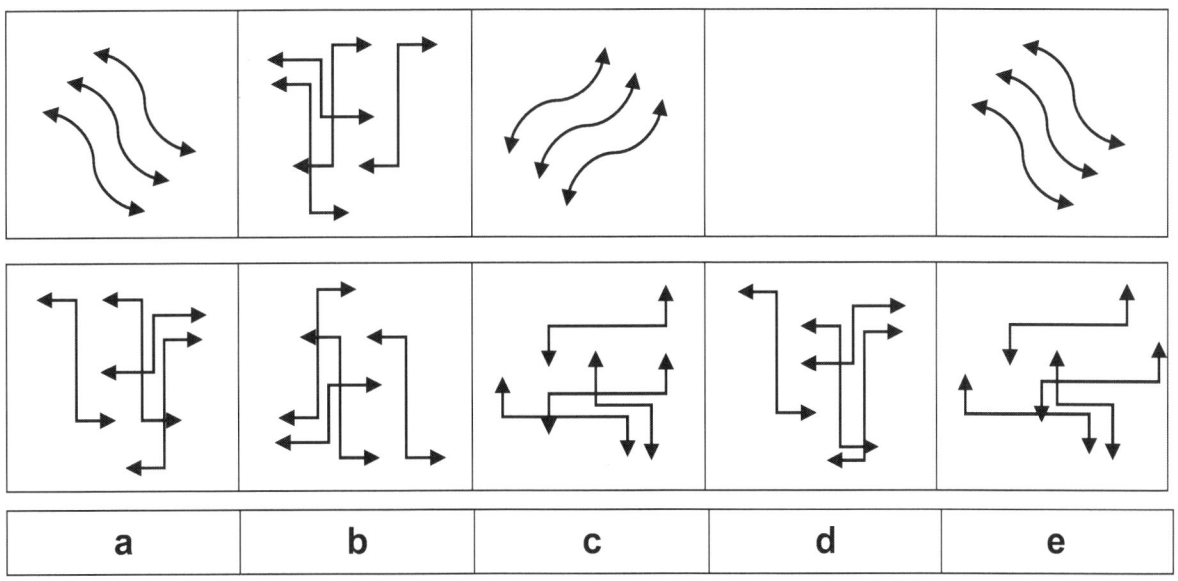

Question 3.4

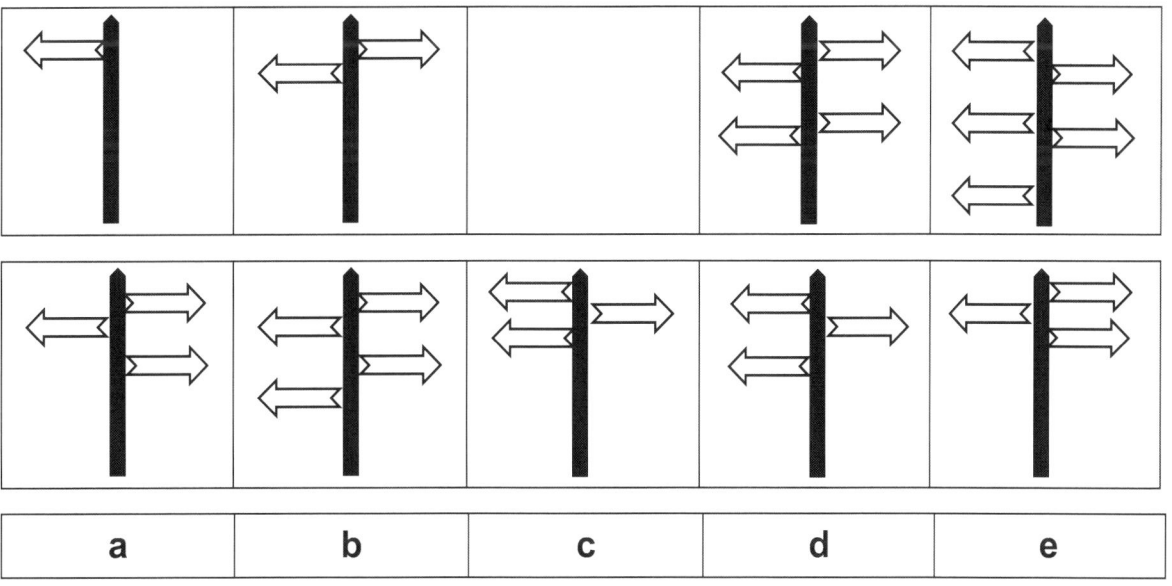

Question 3.5

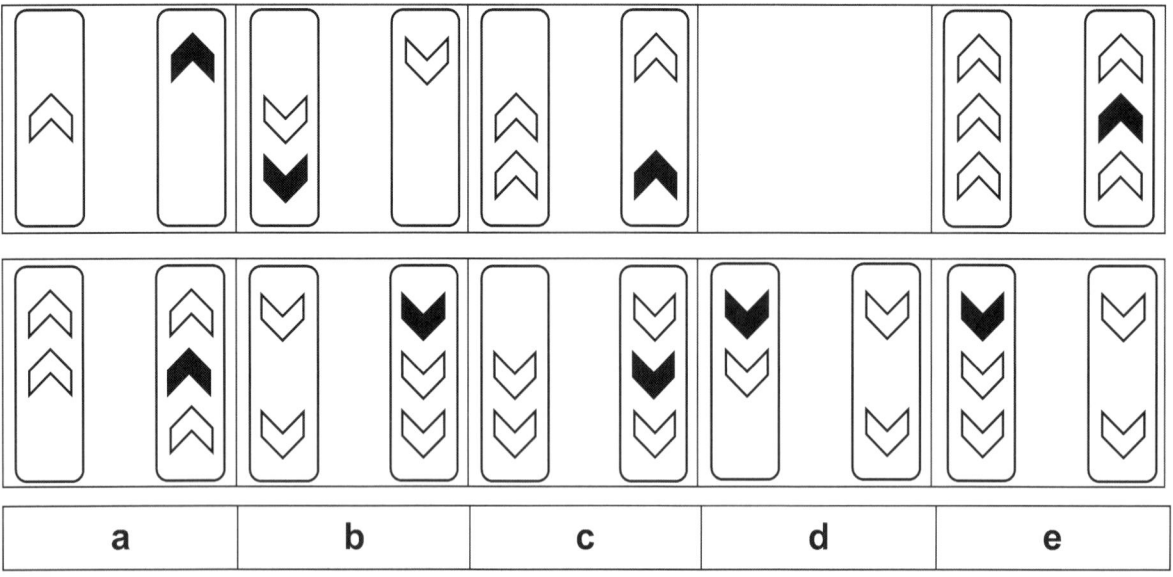

Question 3.6

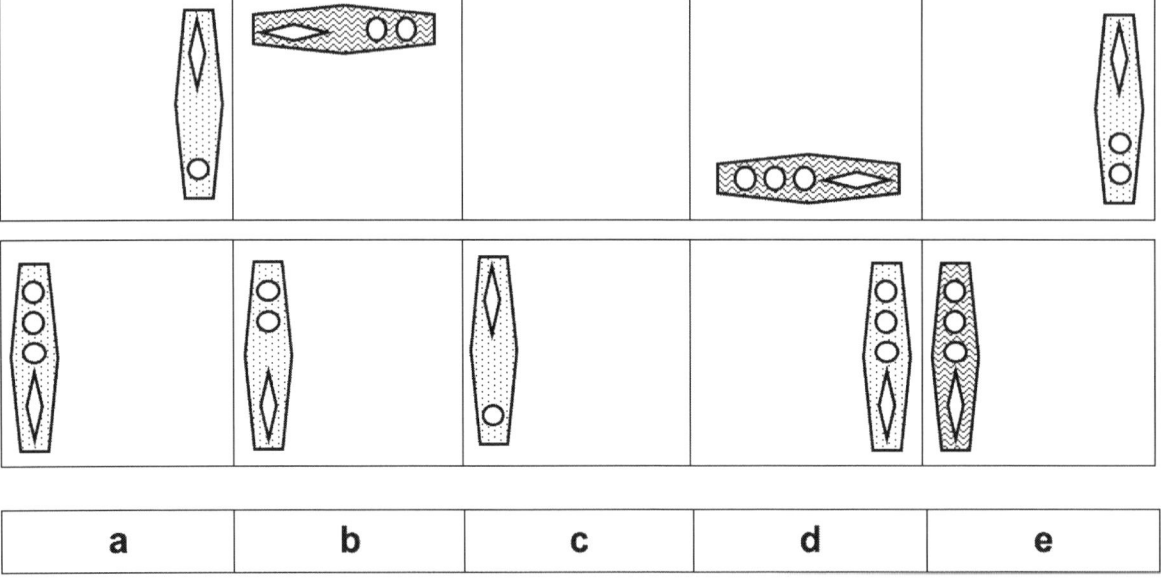

Question 3.7

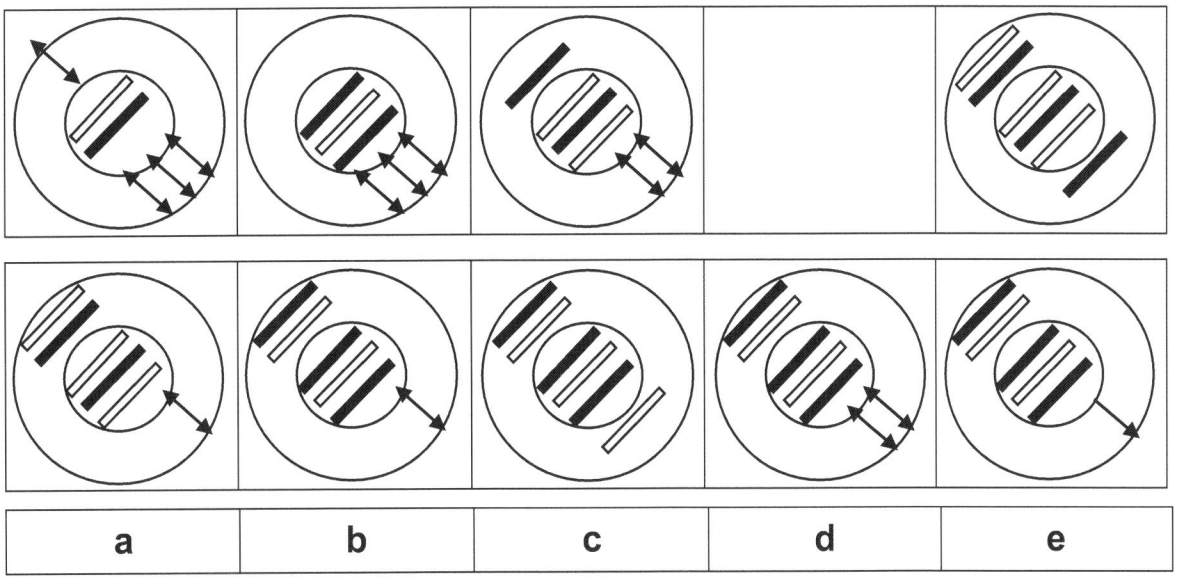

Question 3.8

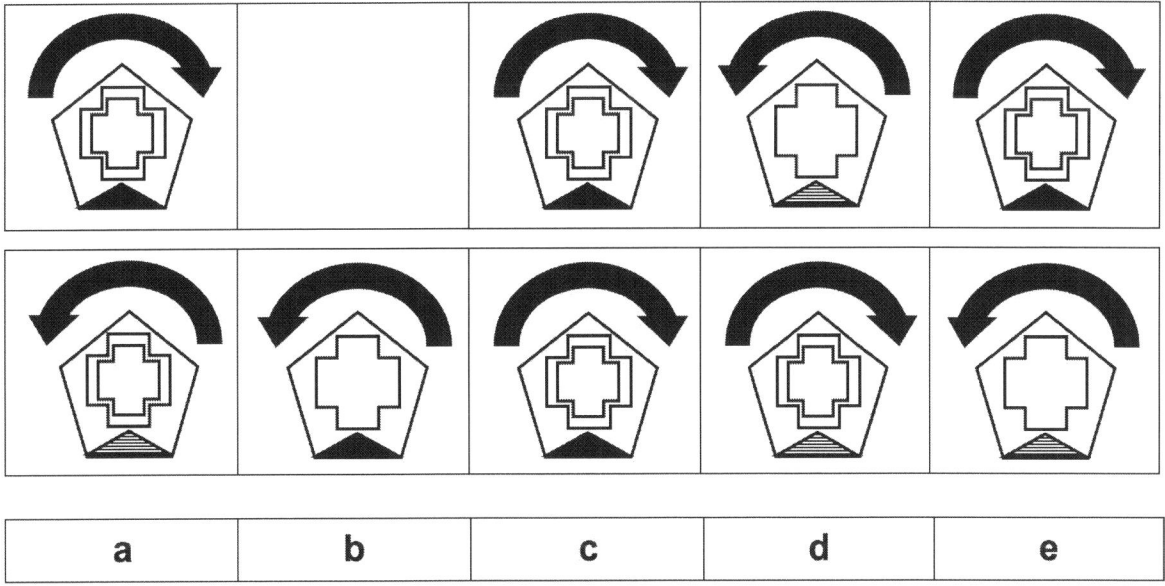

Question 3.9

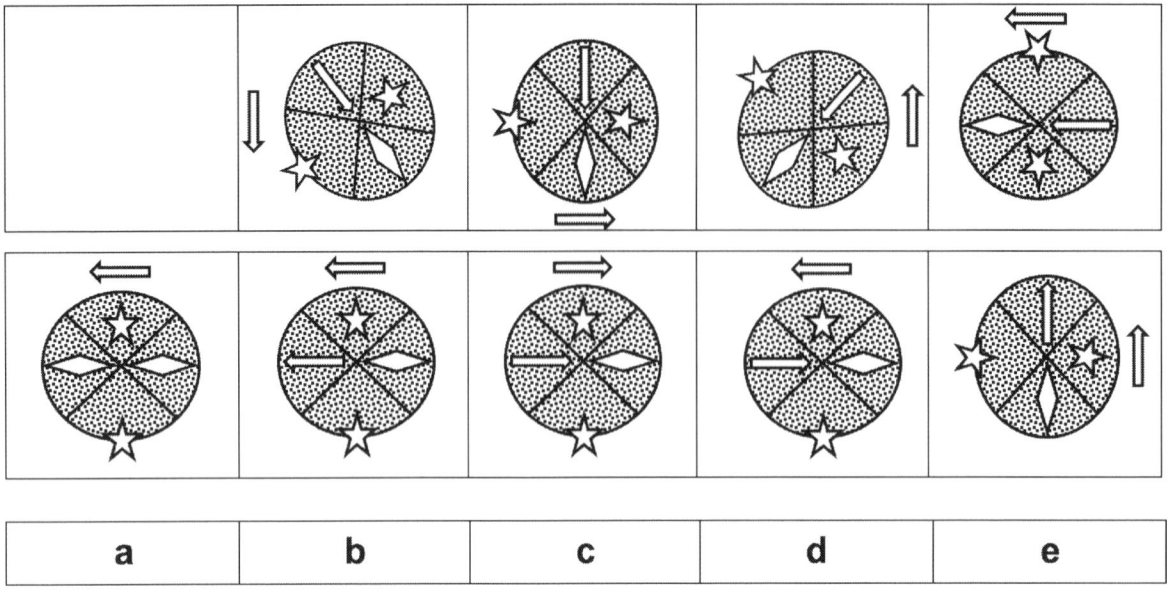

a	b	c	d	e

Question 3.10

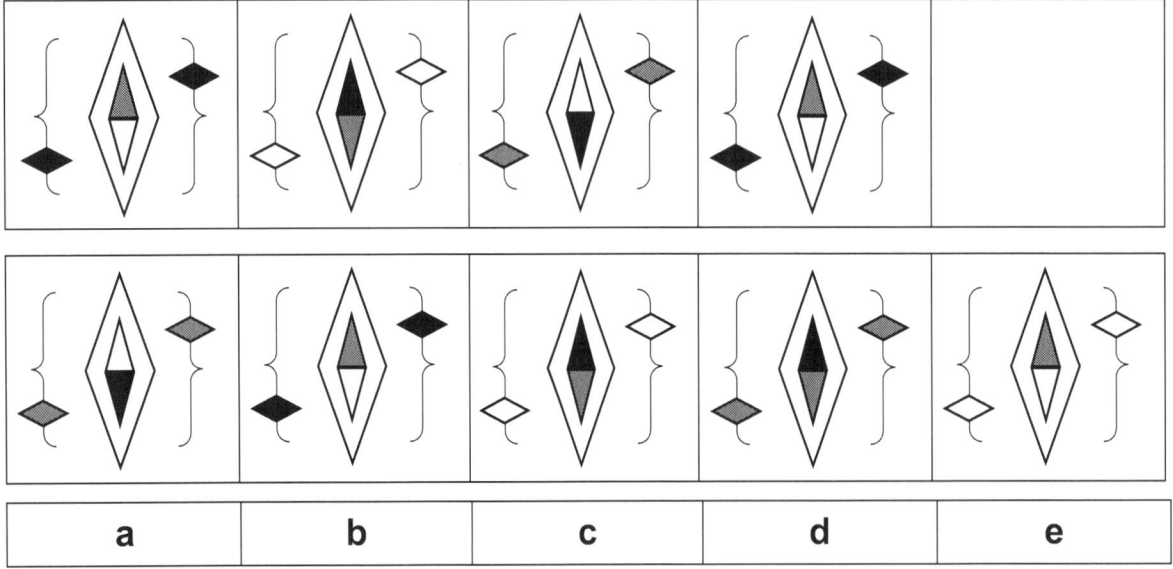

a	b	c	d	e

Question 3.11

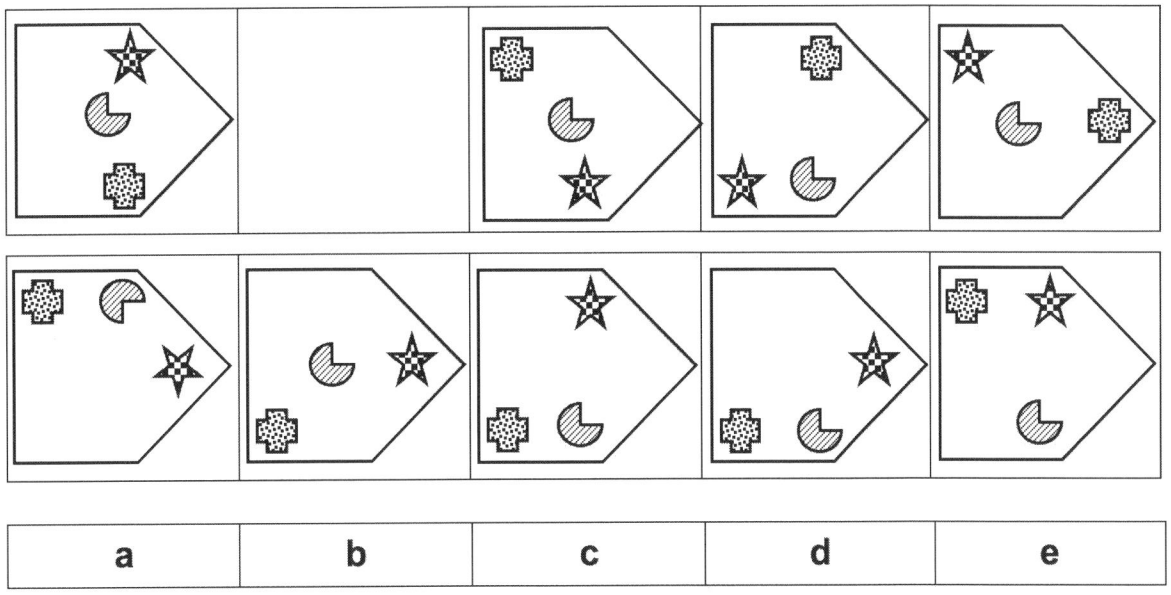

| a | b | c | d | e |

Question 3.12

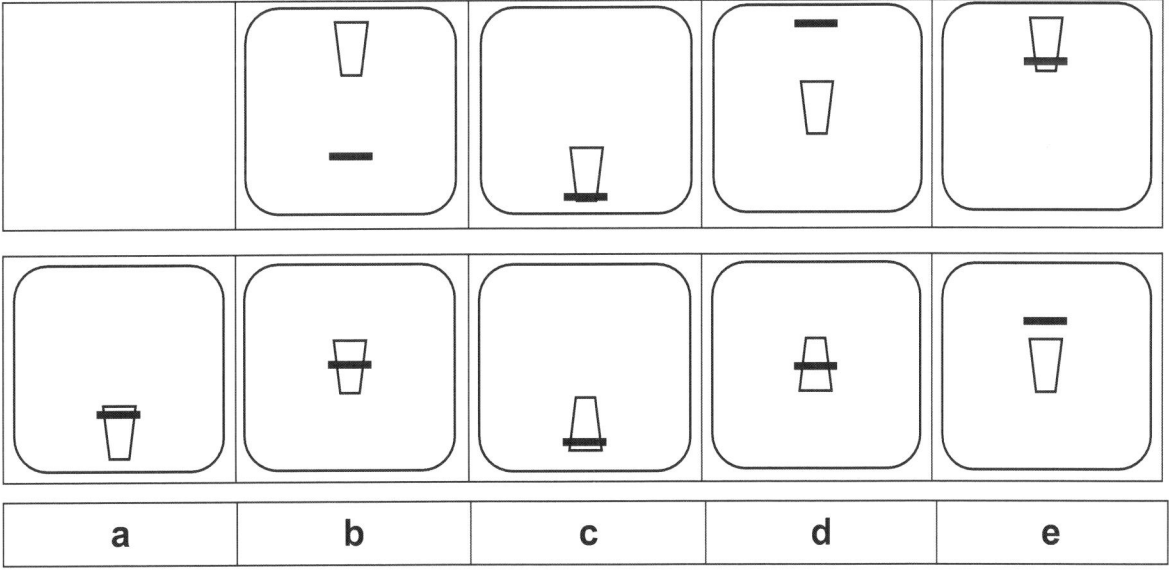

| a | b | c | d | e |

Question 3.13

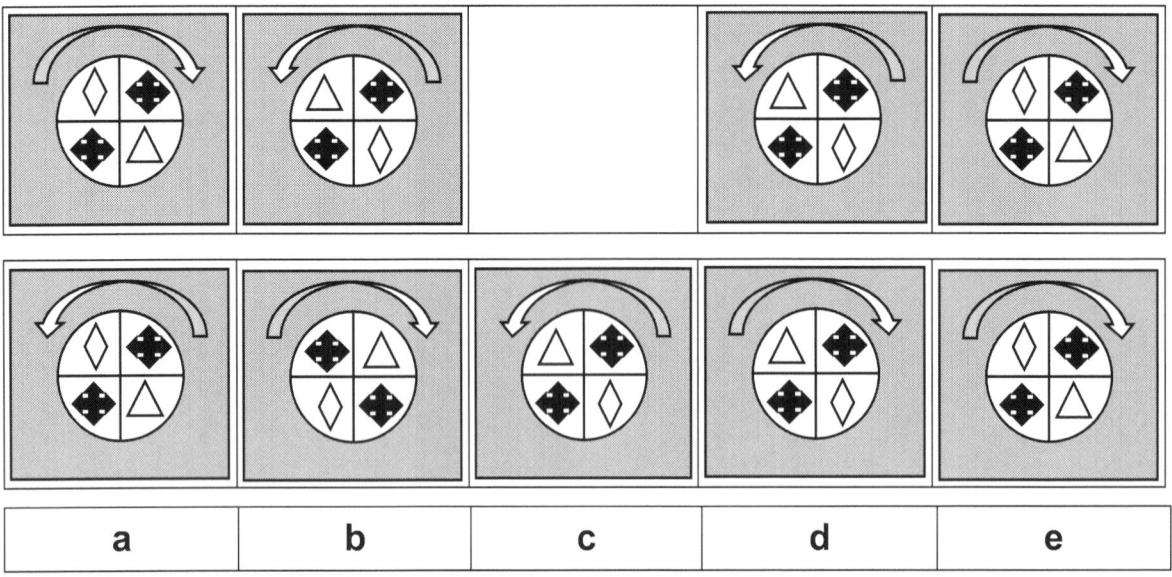

a	b	c	d	e

Question 3.14

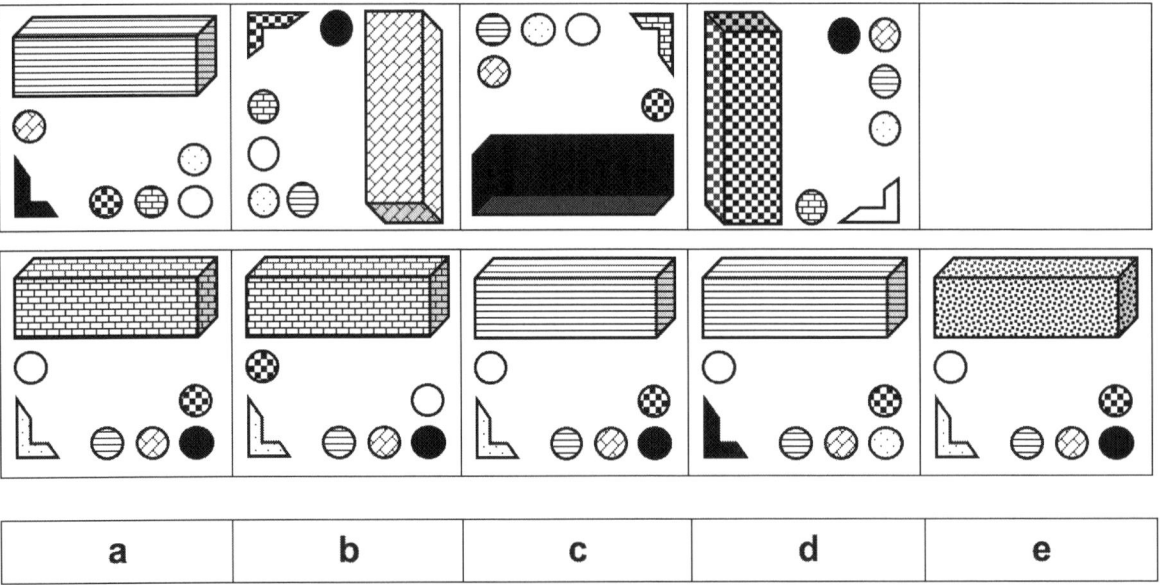

a	b	c	d	e

Question 3.15

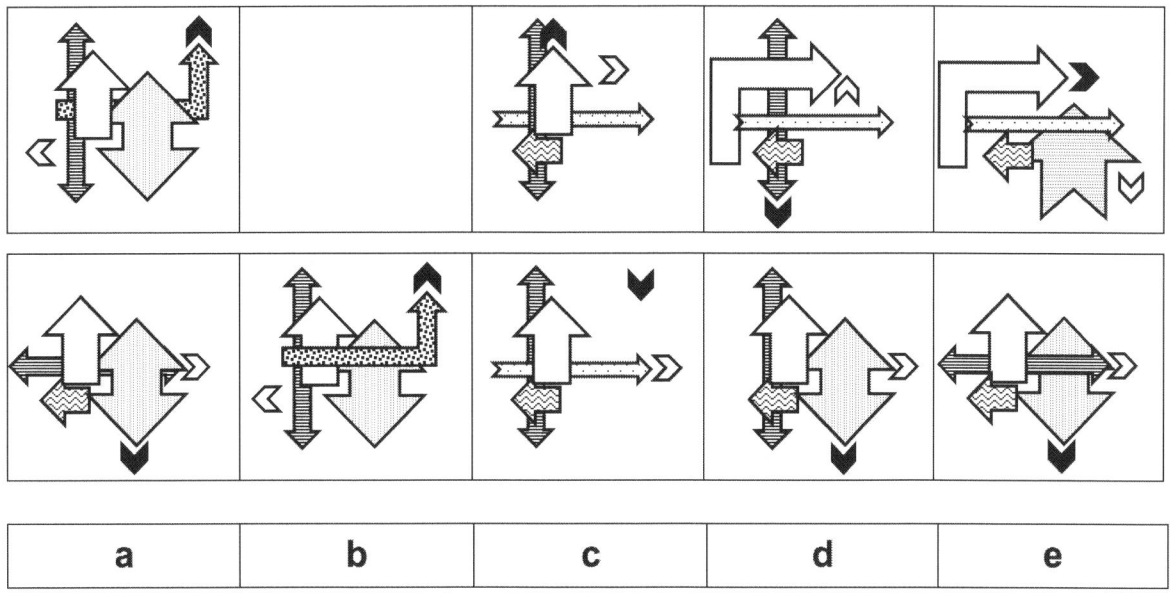

| a | b | c | d | e |

Question 3.16

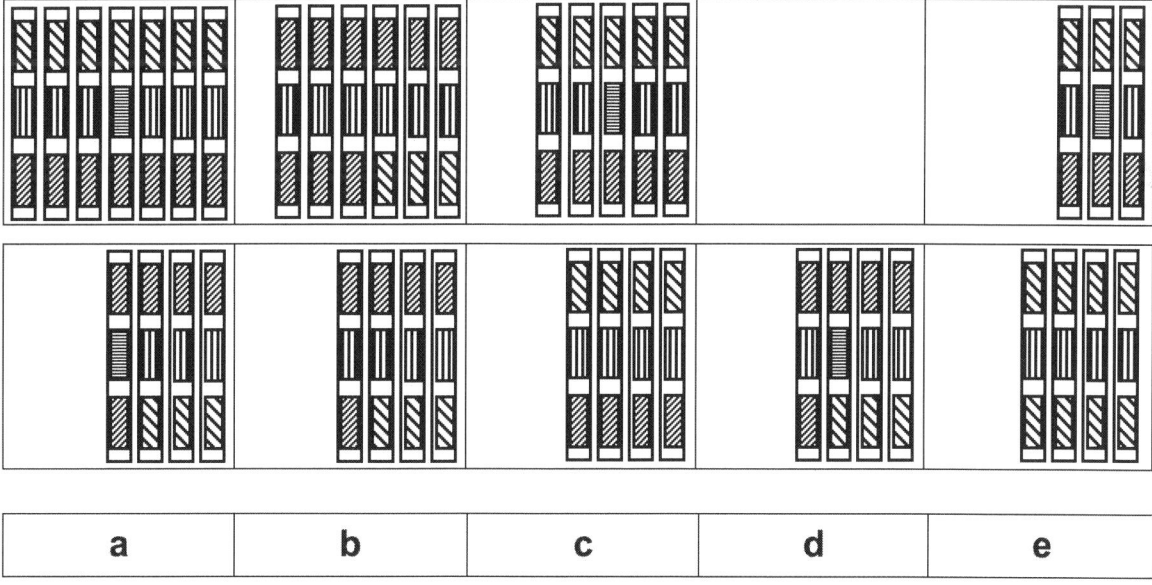

| a | b | c | d | e |

Question 3.17

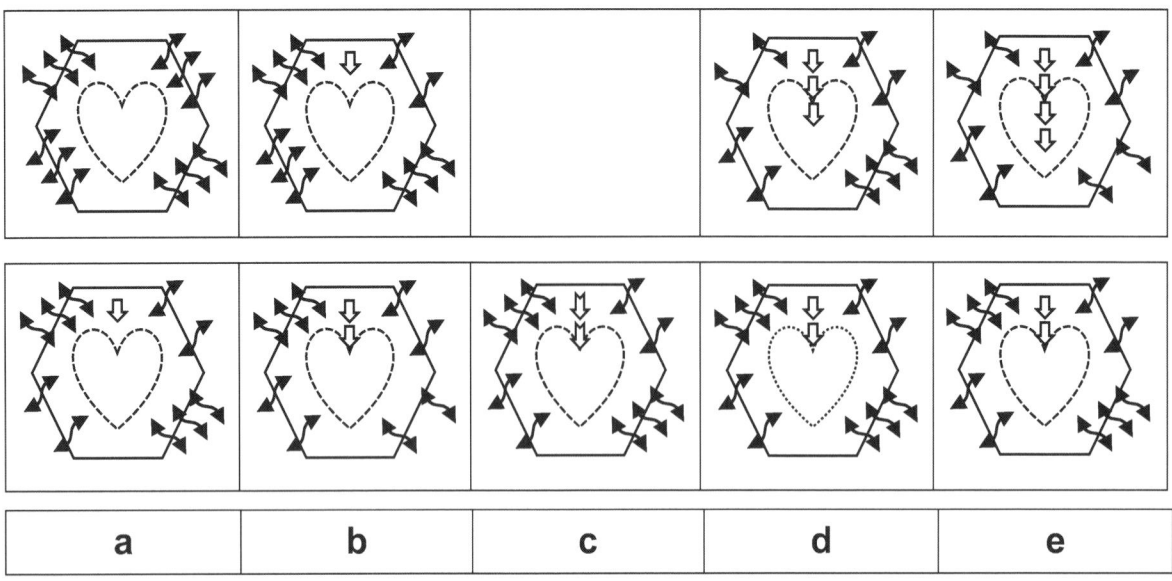

Question 3.18

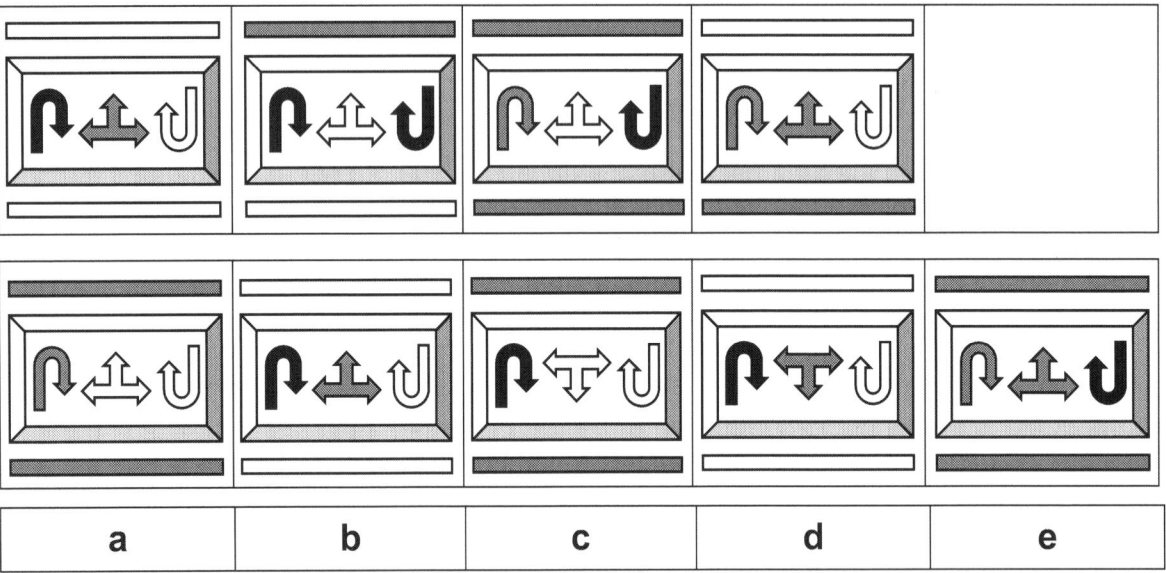

Type 3 Answers

3.1	E	Shape rotates clockwise
3.2	C	Oval alternates from horizontal to vertical. Part circle rotates by 90 degrees clockwise
3.3	A	Wavy lines alternate with straight lines. As the wavy lines alternate they mirror, therefore the straight lines mirror.
3.4	D	Arrows on the left hand side move to right. Arrows on left move up and down Left side adds one arrow one place further down.
3.5	E	Arrows point up and down. Black arrow signals where a new white arrow will appear.
3.6	A	Shape rotates anticlockwise. Shape fill alternates. Spots increase to three then decrease.
3.7	B	Amount of arrows decrease. Amount of lines increase building up from the top then the bottom. Colour of lines swap.
3.8	E	Arrow swaps direction. Triangle alternates between black and striped. Central cross is single or double alternately.
3.9	D	Outside arrow moves anticlockwise. Shape and smaller shapes move as one in a clockwise direction.
3.10	C	All shapes change colour in the same sequence.
3.11	D	There are six "positions" inside the main shape. Star moves one position each time. Cross moves one position each time. Part circle moves between two positions each time
3.12	B	There are three "positions" for the cup: top, middle and bottom. There are five "positions" for the line. The line moves down then up again.
3.13	E	Arrow swaps direction. Black squares with spots remain in the same position. Diamond and triangle swap places.
3.14	A	Cuboid and other shapes move as one, clockwise. There must be one of each fill: Black, Diagonal bricks, Horizontal bricks, Chequered, Lines, White and Spotted. Fills rotate in order.
3.15	D	A black arrowhead signals which arrow is going to disappear. A white arrowhead signals where an arrow is going to appear.
3.16	B	Rectangles decrease by one from the left hand side. A horizontal rectangle appears alternately in the middle section. Top patterns alternate. Bottom pattern alternates.
3.17	E	Tiny arrows increase from top down. Double ended arrows decrease from top right, then bottom left, then top left and then bottom right.
3.18	B	Outside thin rectangles changes colour in twos. Middle three ended arrow changes colour in twos. Curved arrow changes colour in twos

Type 4

What is the missing image in each matrix?

Question 4.1

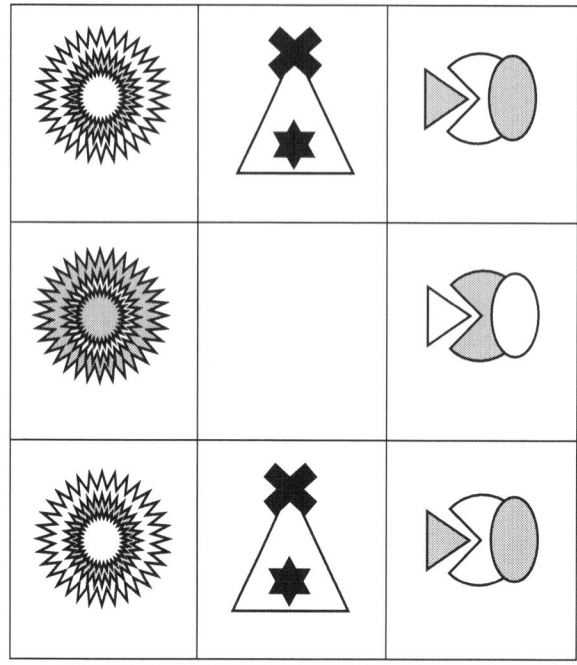

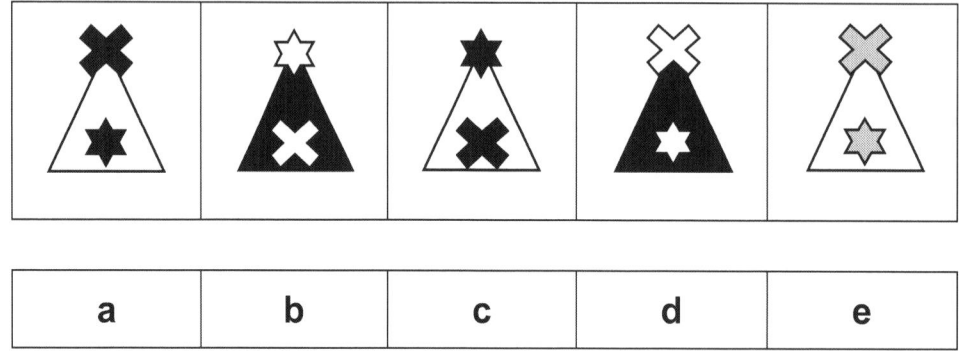

| a | b | c | d | e |

Question 4.2

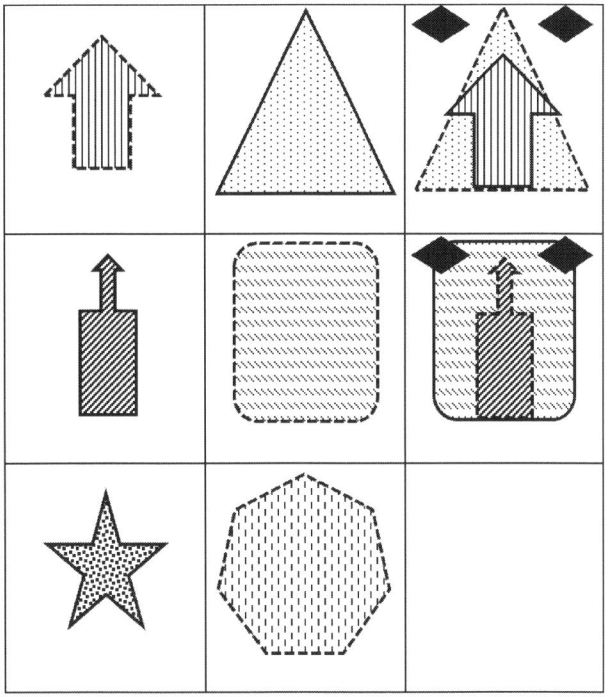

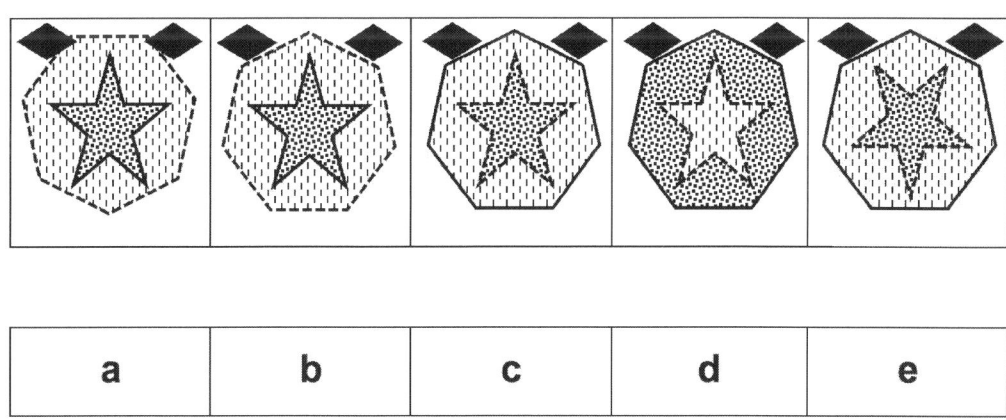

a	b	c	d	e

Question 4.3

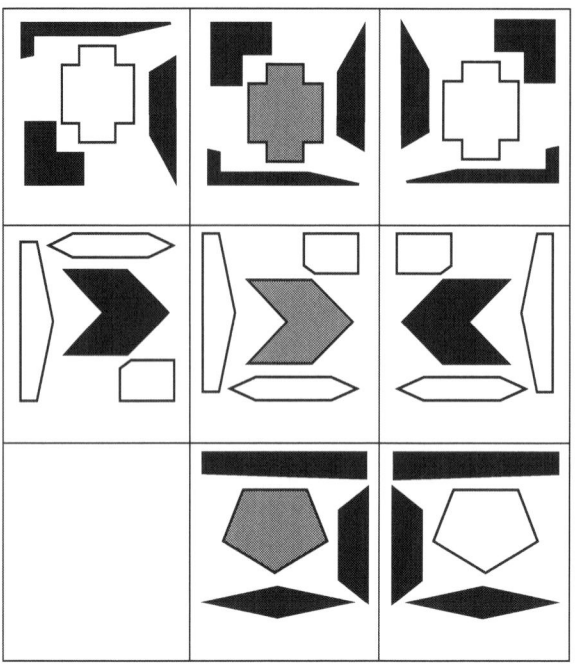

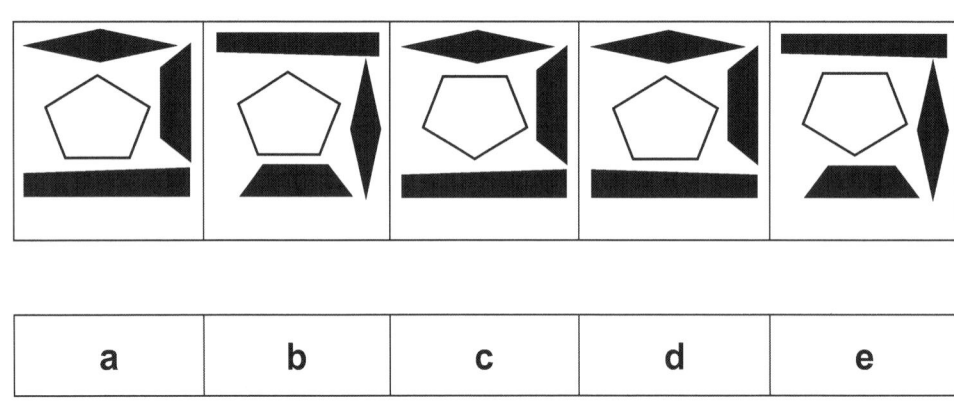

| a | b | c | d | e |

Question 4.4

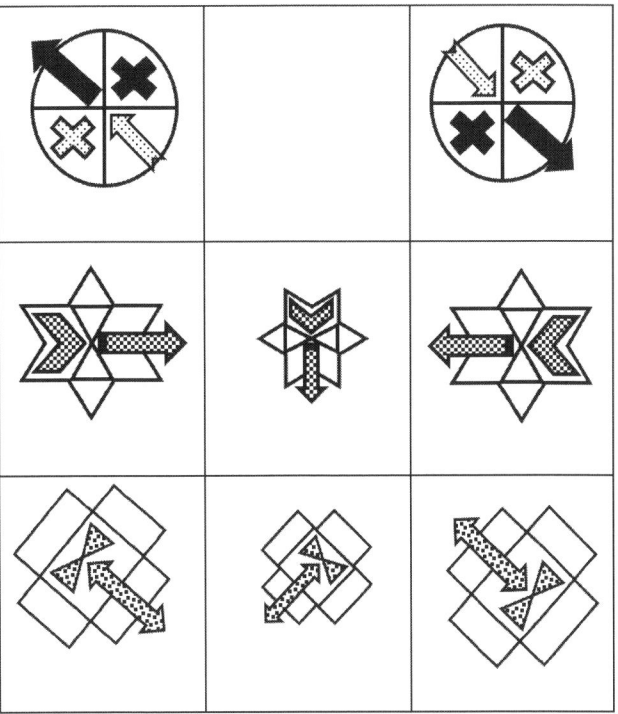

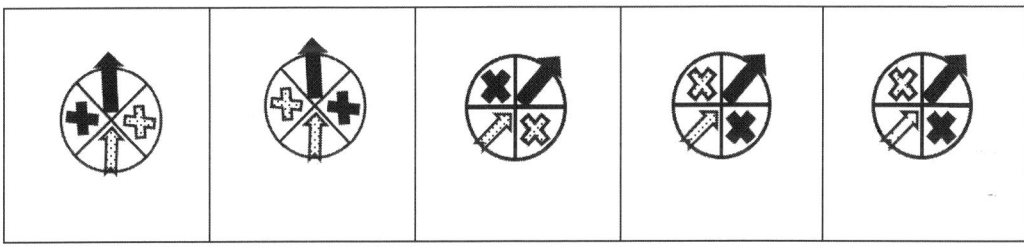

a	b	c	d	e

Question 4.5

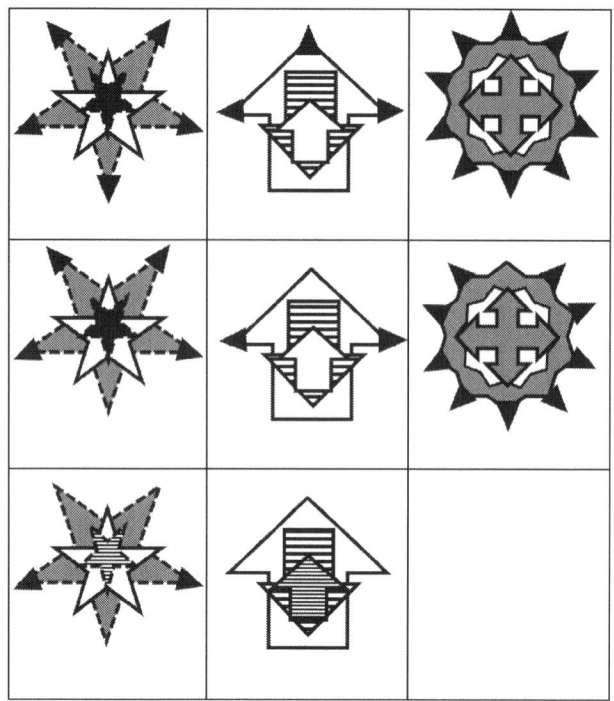

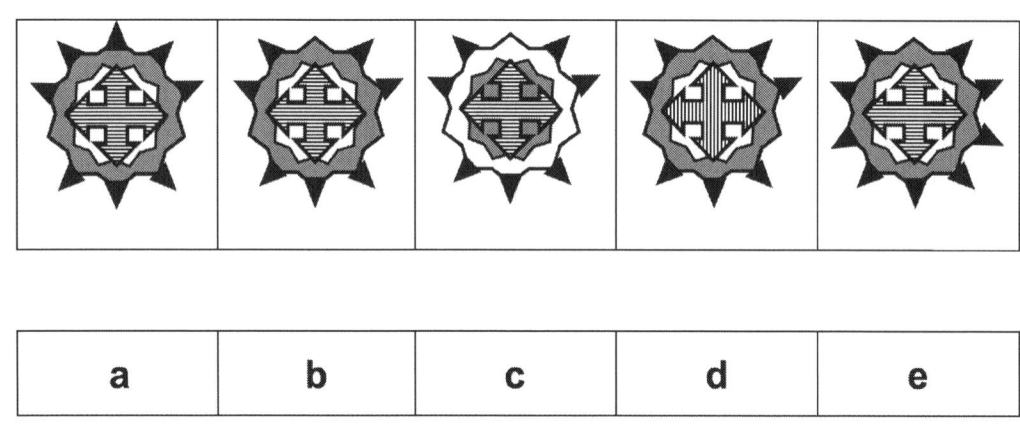

a	b	c	d	e

Question 4.6

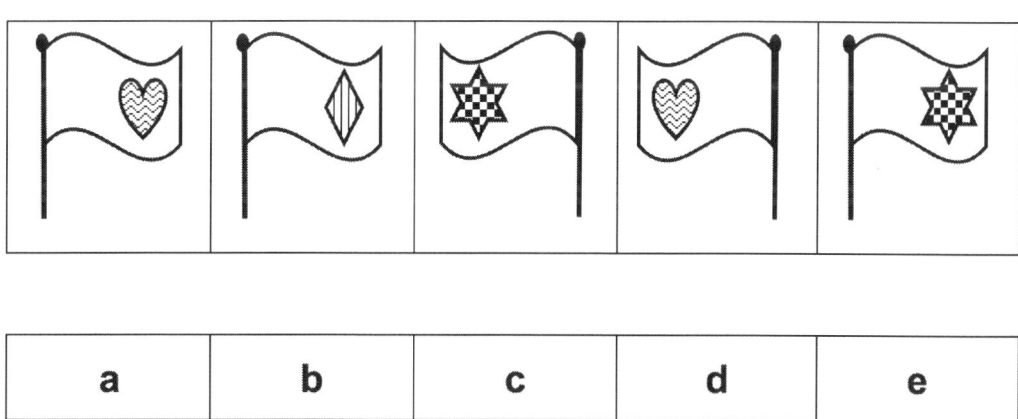

a	b	c	d	e

Question 4.7

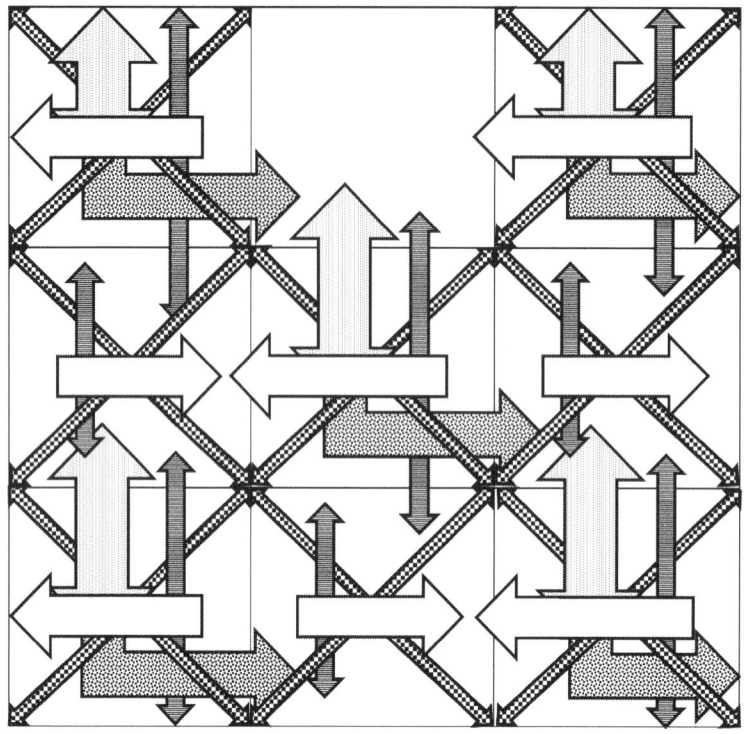

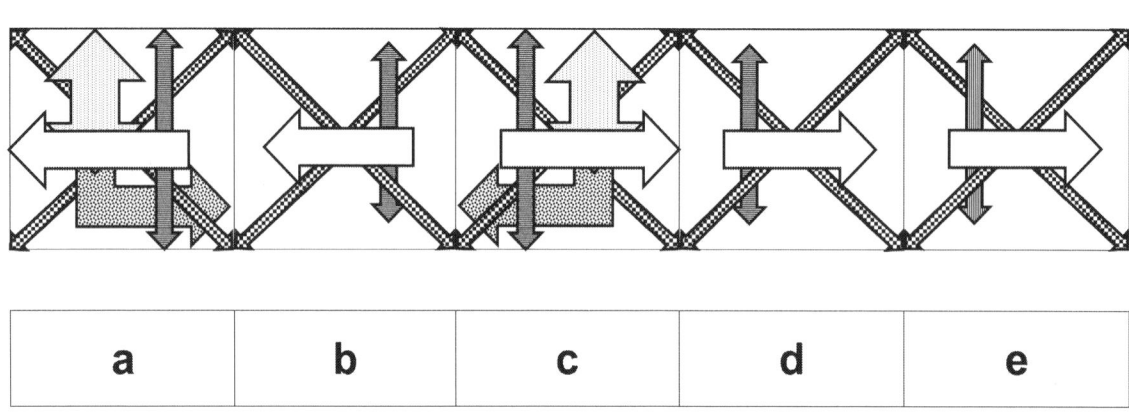

a	b	c	d	e

Question 4.8

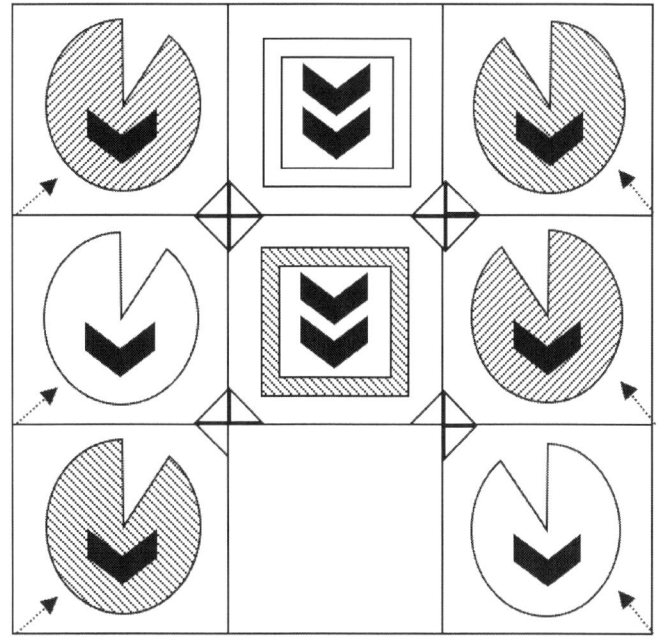

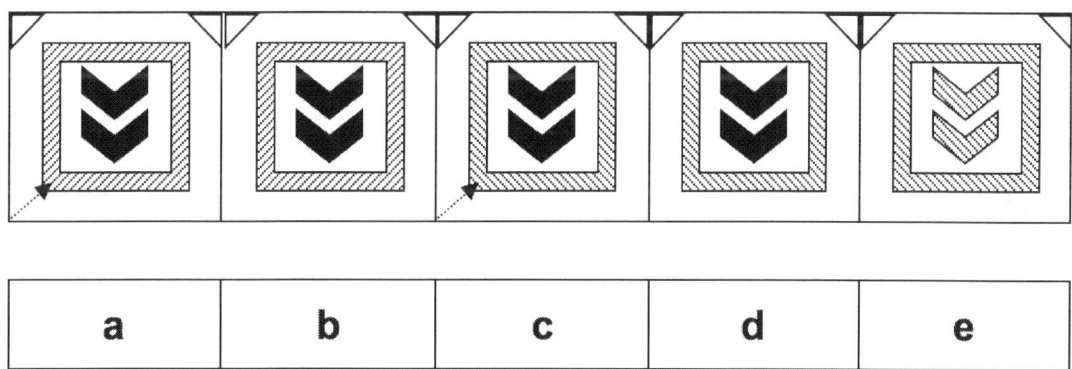

a	b	c	d	e

Question 4.9

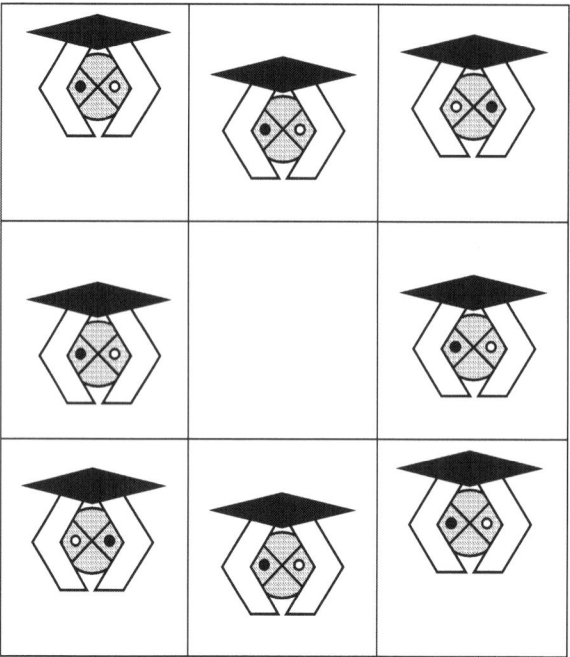

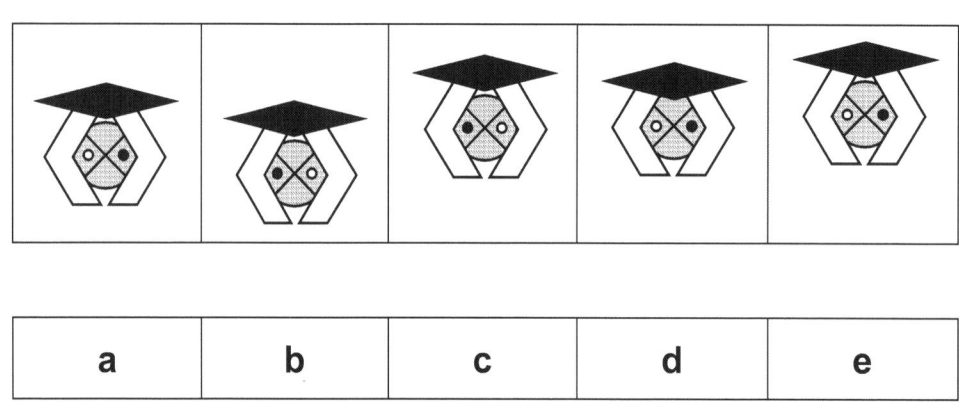

Question 4.10

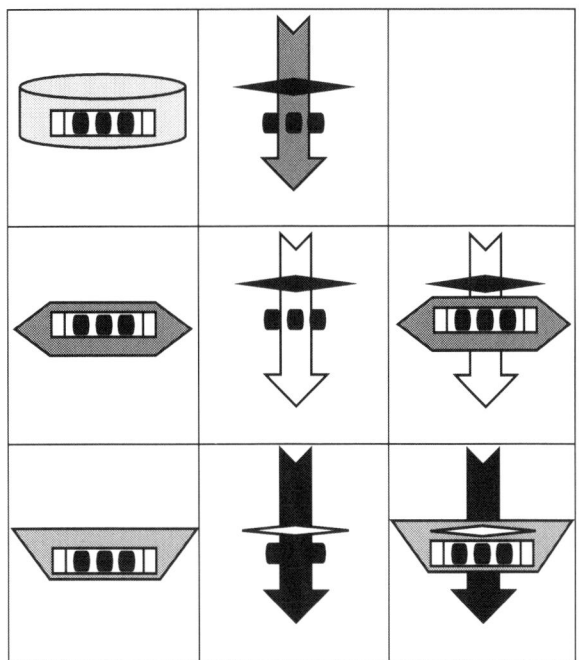

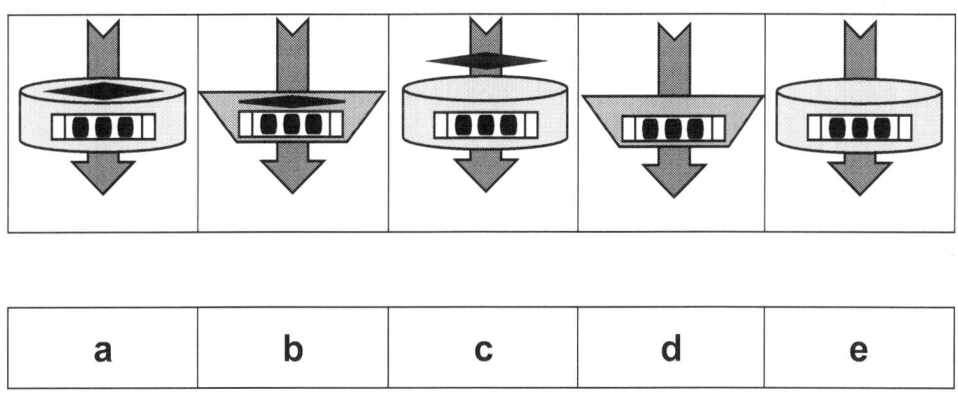

| a | b | c | d | e |

Question 4.11

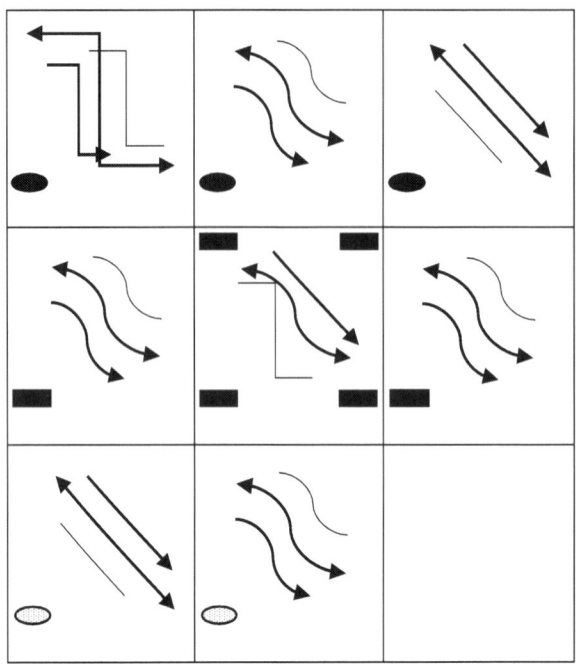

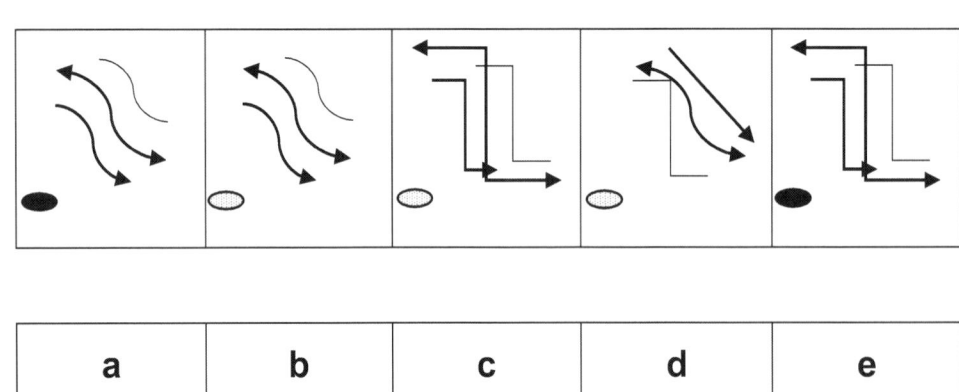

| a | b | c | d | e |

Question 4.12

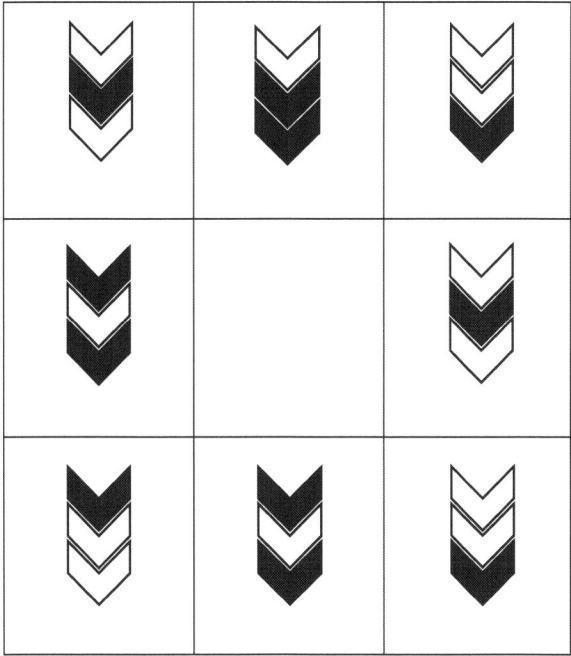

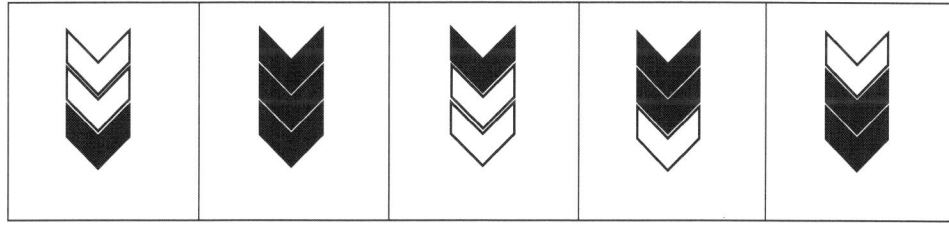

a	b	c	d	e

Question 4.13

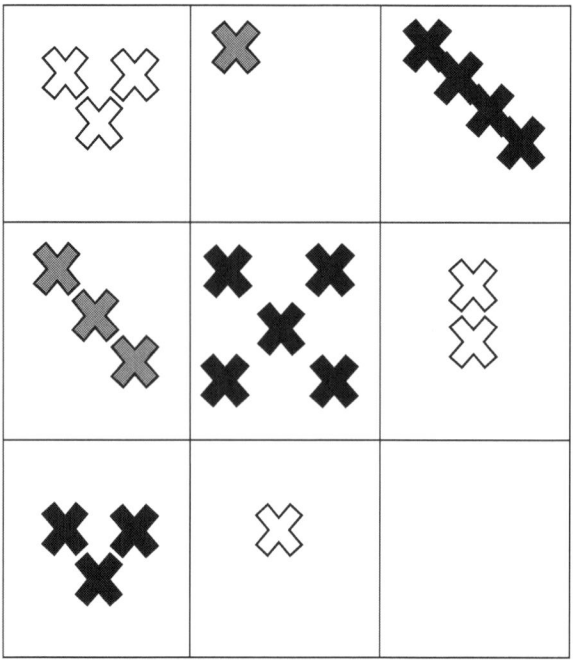

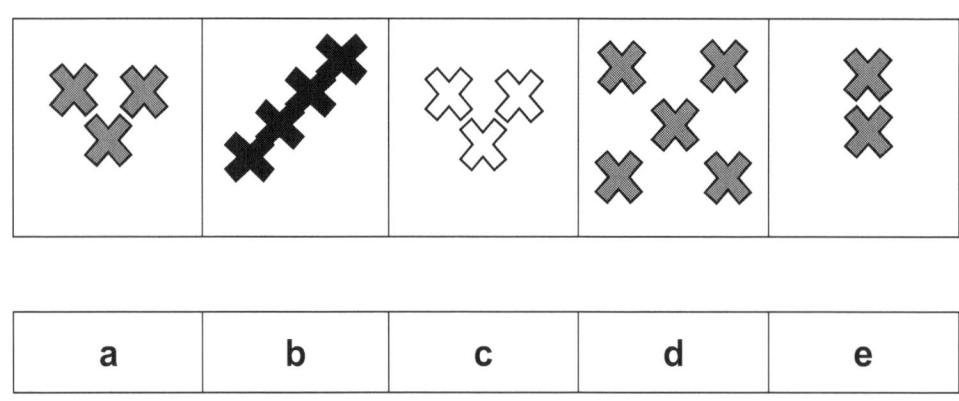

| a | b | c | d | e |

Question 4.14

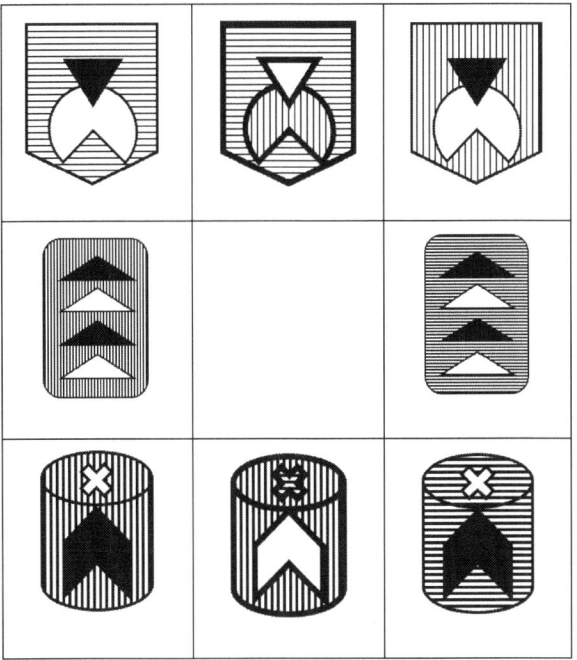

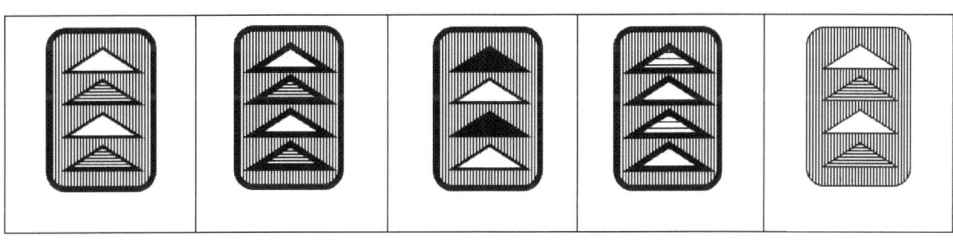

| a | b | c | d | e |

Question 4.15

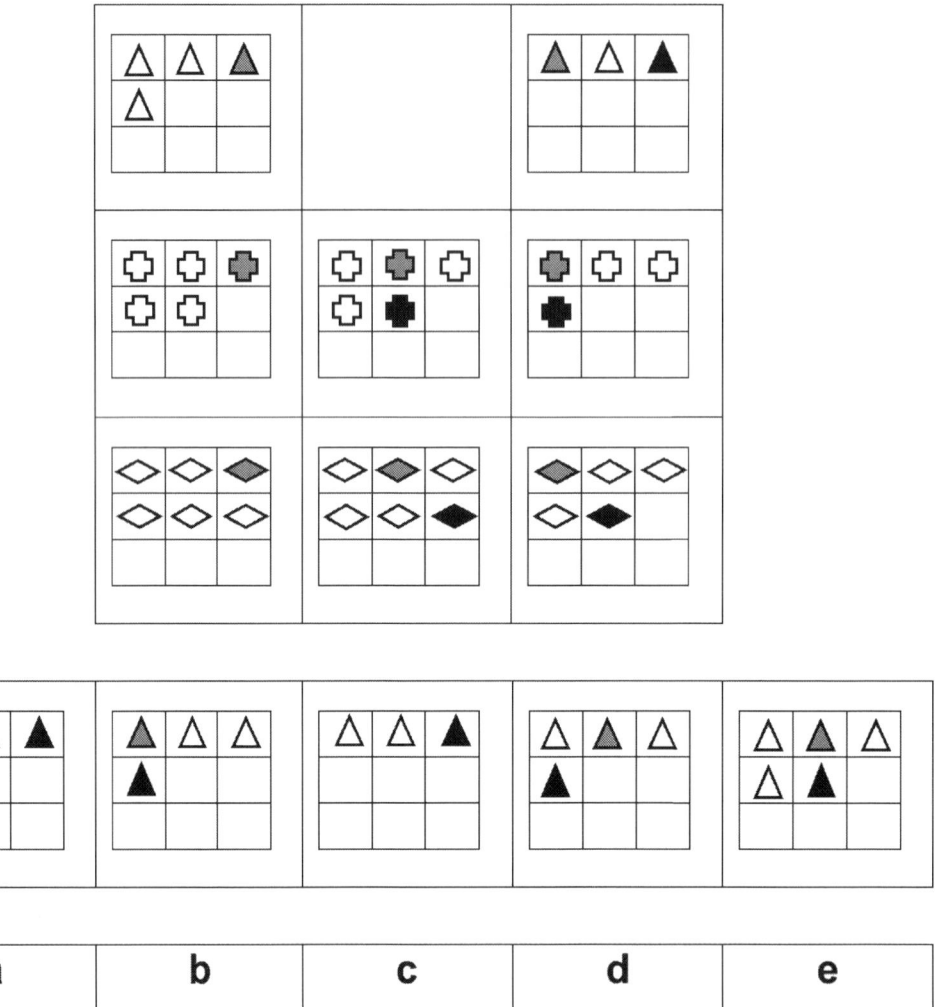

| a | b | c | d | e |

Question 4.16

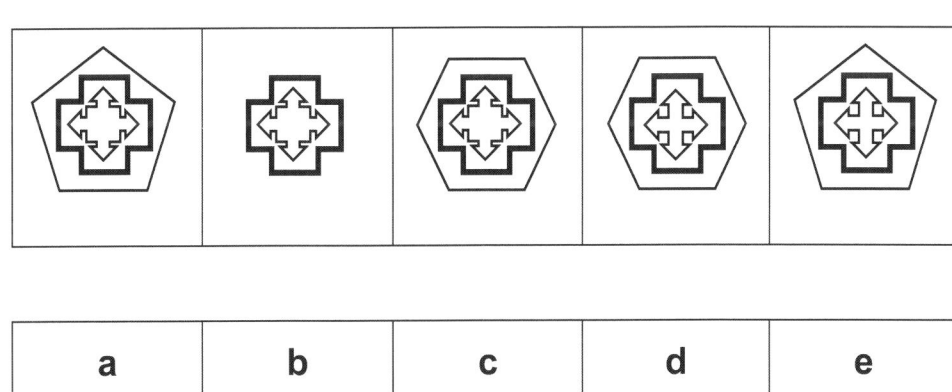

| a | b | c | d | e |

Type 4 Answers

4.1	D	Top and bottom colour in each column are the same. Colours swap in vertical middle row images.
4.2	C	Images in left and middle column combine to make images in right hand column. Two black diamonds are added. Dashed lines change to solid and vice versa.
4.3	A	Centre and right hand column are mirror images of each other. Centre shape turns grey. Right hand column image has been flipped vertically then flipped horizontally to create left hand column image. Colours remain the same.
4.4	C	The top and bottom row corners are produced when image is flipped vertically & horizontally. Middle column of top and bottom row are smaller mirror images of left hand column. The centre square has its own rules.
4.5	B	Bottom row small centre shapes have vertical stripes. Top row: all triangles. Middle row: decreases by one triangle. Bottom row: decreases by two more triangles.
4.6	E	Top and bottom rows are flags. Smaller images are repeated diagonally from the left hand column. Shapes in left and right hand column face the same way.
4.7	D	White arrows are repeated in direction diagonally from the left hand column. Thin double-ended arrow, horizontally striped.
4.8	B	All arrowheads are black. Arrows with broken lines are on left and right hand columns only. Diagonal fill is mirror image. One image on each row must be white.
4.9	E	Coloured dot formation is repeated diagonally from top right column. Whole image is in the same vertical position.
4.10	A	Images in left and middle column combine to make images in right hand column.
4.11	C	Small shape in bottom left hand corner repeats in each row. Diagonal corners are the same image. Middle image has different rule. Middle of top and bottom row and first and third images in row two are the same image.
4.12	B	The first and third columns combine to make the centre column.
4.13	E	Each row and column has an image of each colour. Each colour image has a consecutive amount of shapes in the whole matrix.
4.14	B	Images in left and right columns are identical except that stripes change from vertical/horizontal to horizontal/vertical. The main stripes in the centre column match the image in the left hand column. The lines in the centre column are thicker. In the centre column the images change from black to white. In the centre column the smaller image changes from any colour to a striped image. The stripes are different to the background stripe.
4.15	D	Small shapes repeat in each row. The amount of small shapes in the centre column is identical to the column on the left. The coloured shapes change position by one each time across the row. The last colour shape in the right and middle column is always black.
4.16	C	The first and third columns combine to make the centre column. In the centre column the hexagon changes to a pentagon.

Type 5

Find the correct net for the cube.

Question 5.1

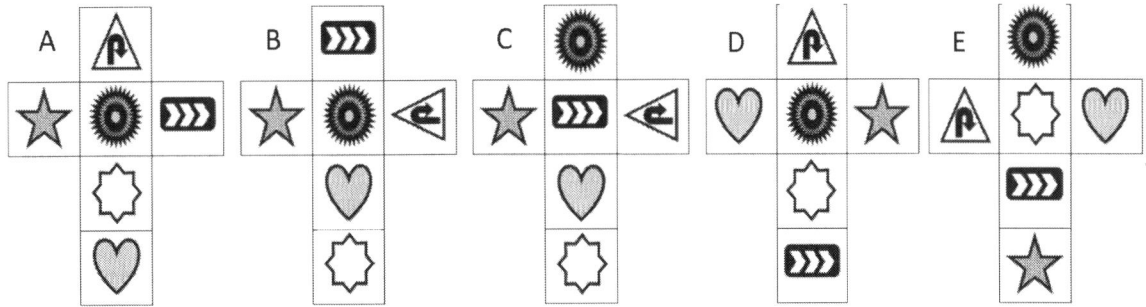

Question 5.2

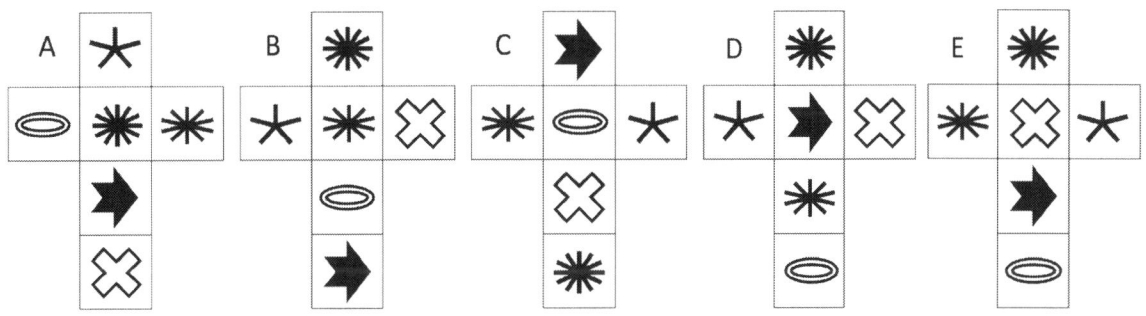

Question 5.3

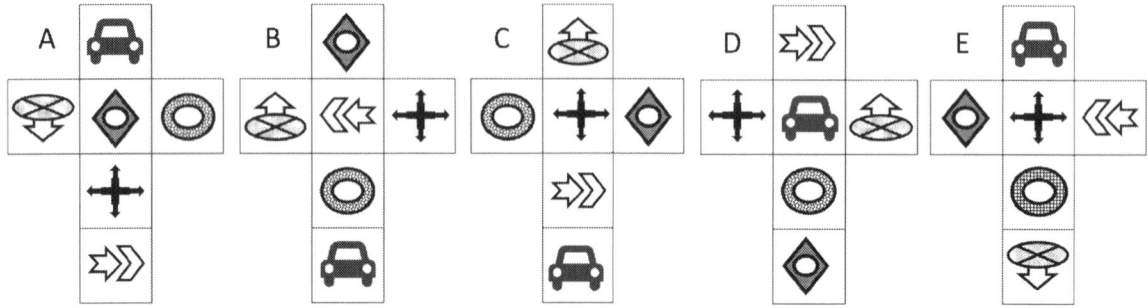

Question 5.4

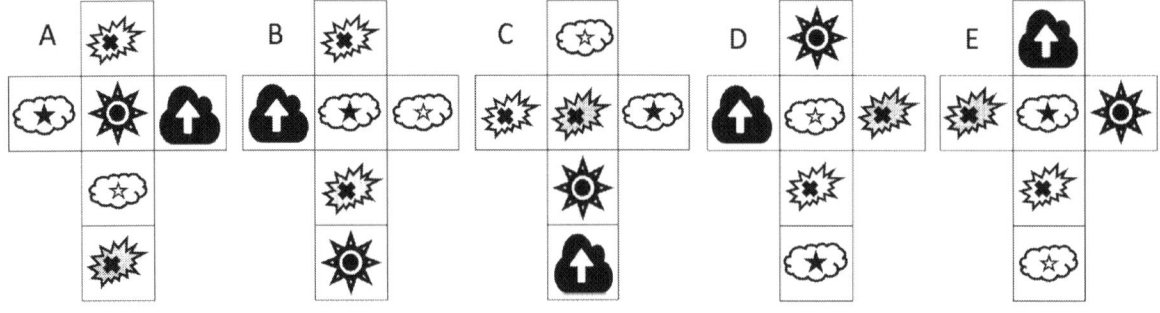

Question 5.5

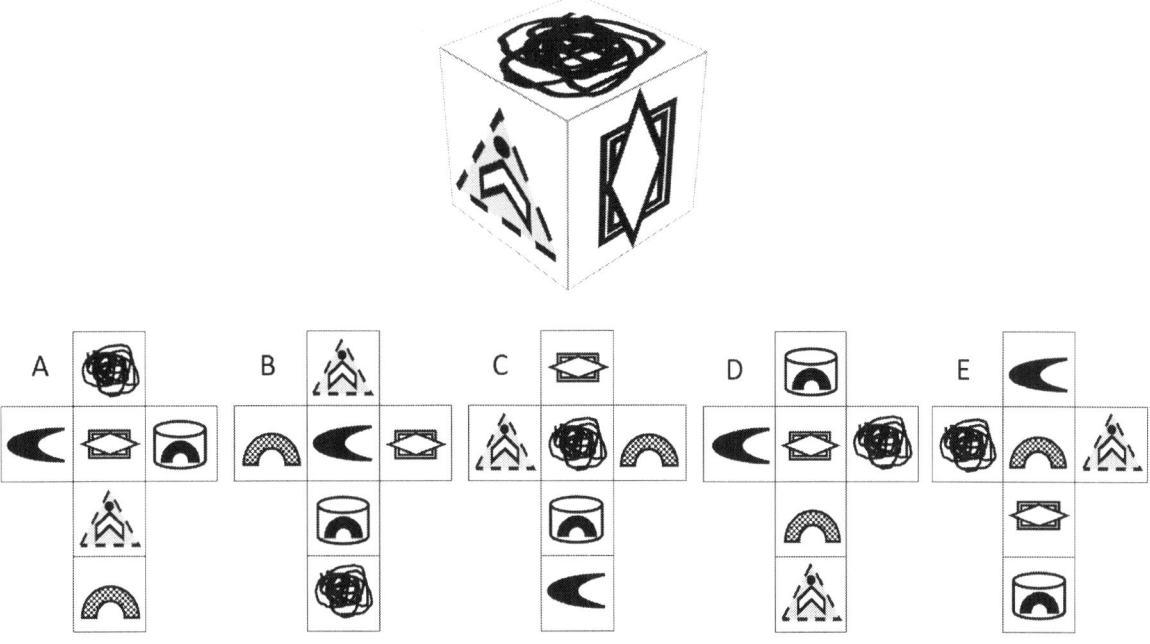

Question 5.6

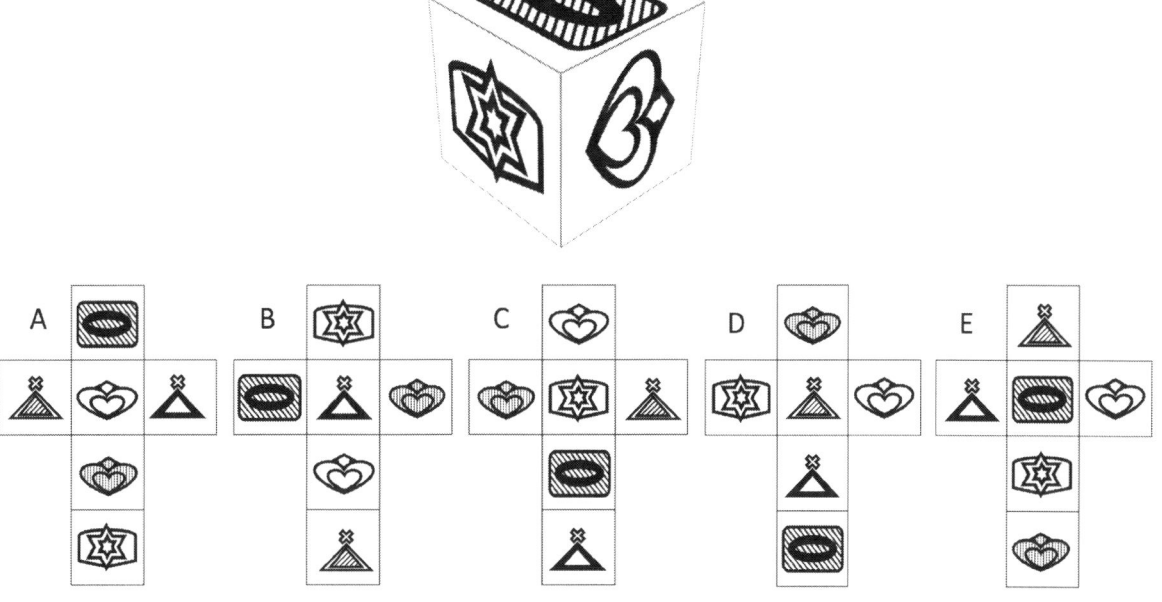

Question 5.7

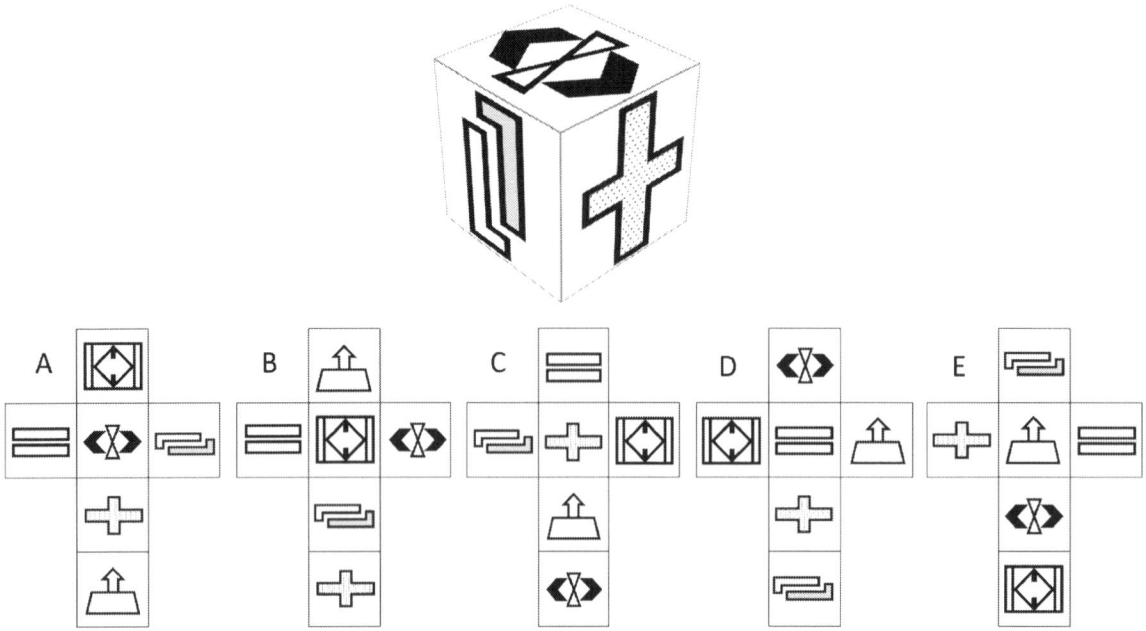

Question 5.8

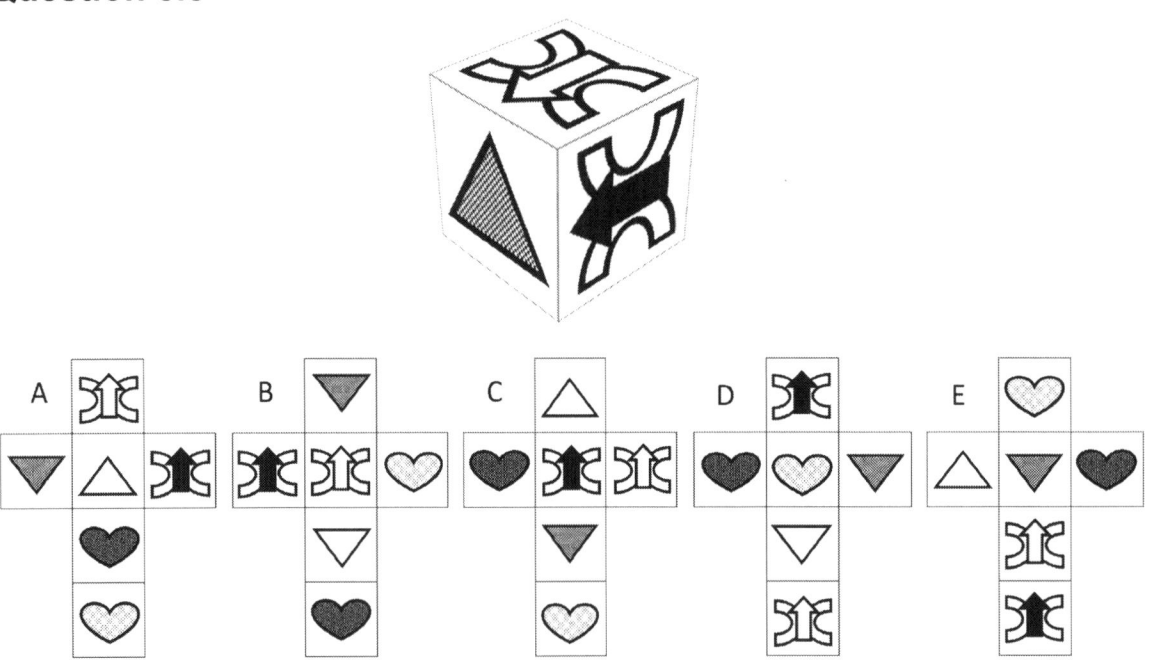

Question 5.9

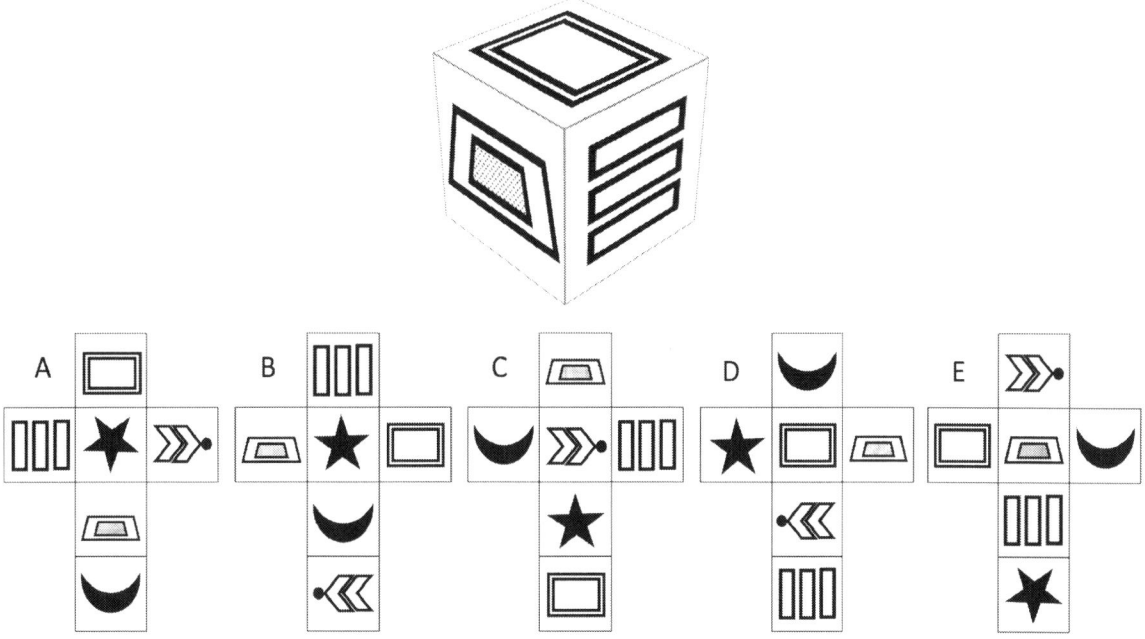

Question 5.10

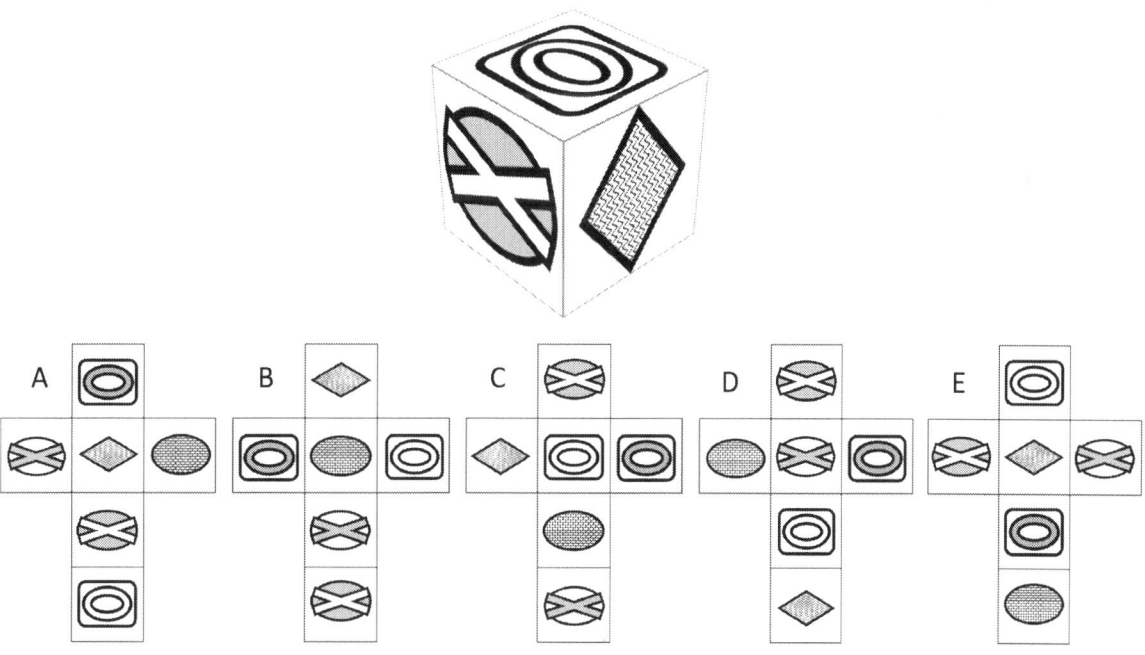

Question 5.11

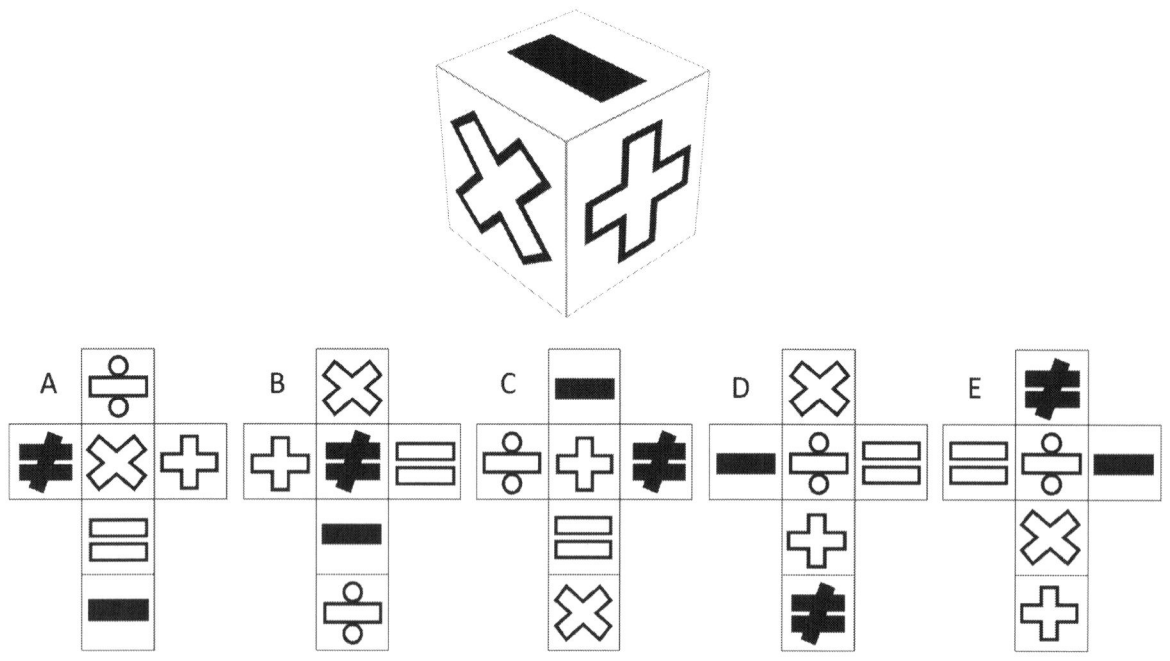

Question 5.12

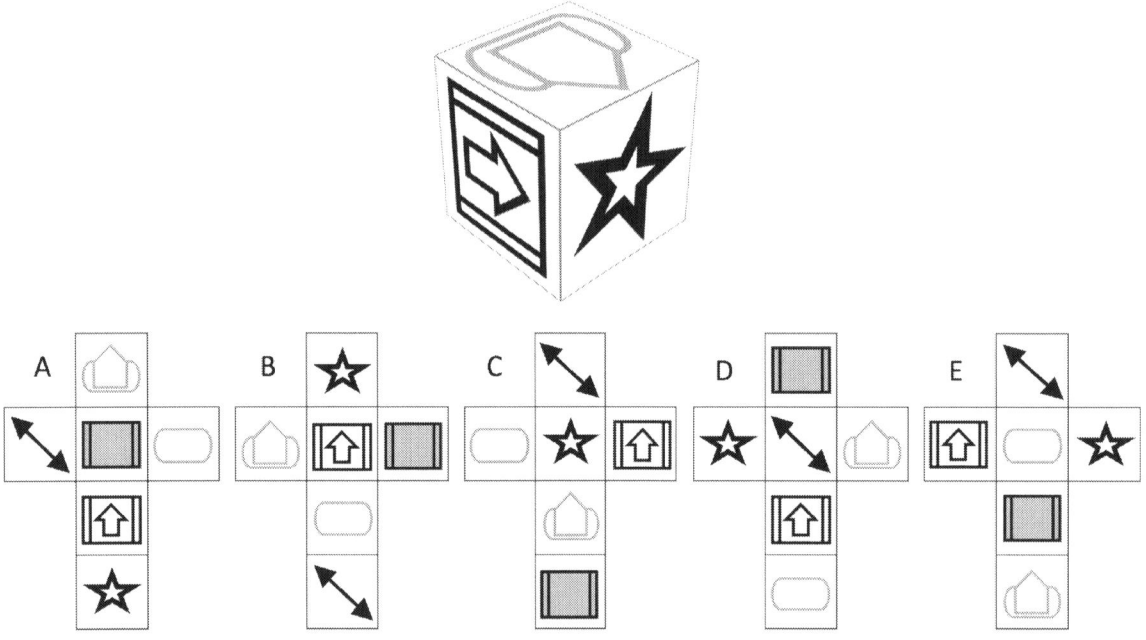

Type 5 Answers

5.1	A
5.2	D
5.3	B
5.4	D
5.5	B
5.6	E
5.7	B
5.8	B
5.9	C
5.10	C
5.11	E
5.12	B

Type 6

The group of cubes has been viewed from above. Which is the correct 2D view?

Question 6.1

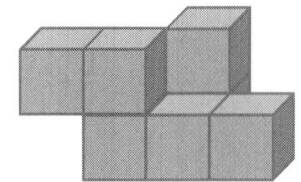

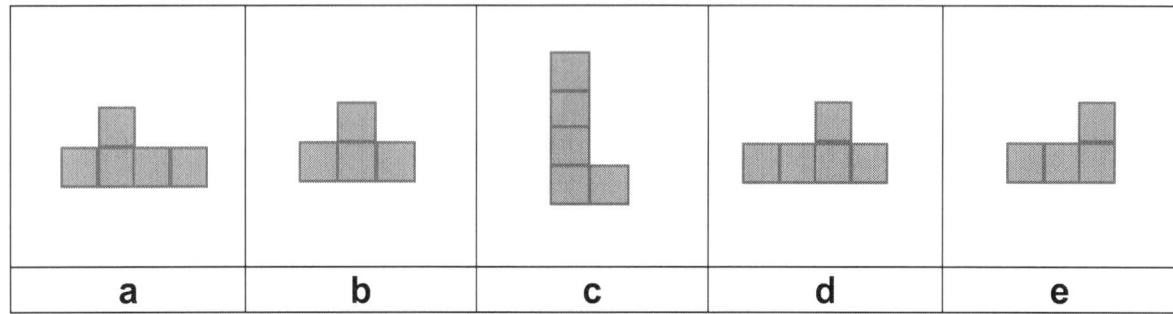

a	b	c	d	e

Question 6.2

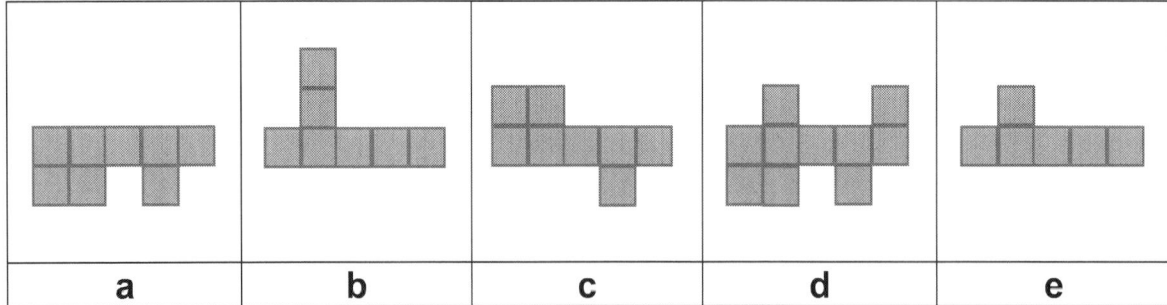

a	b	c	d	e

Question 6.3

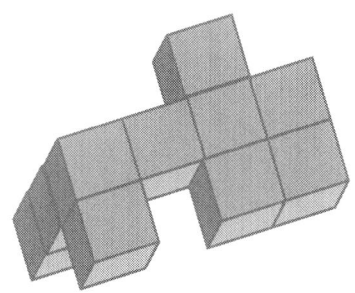

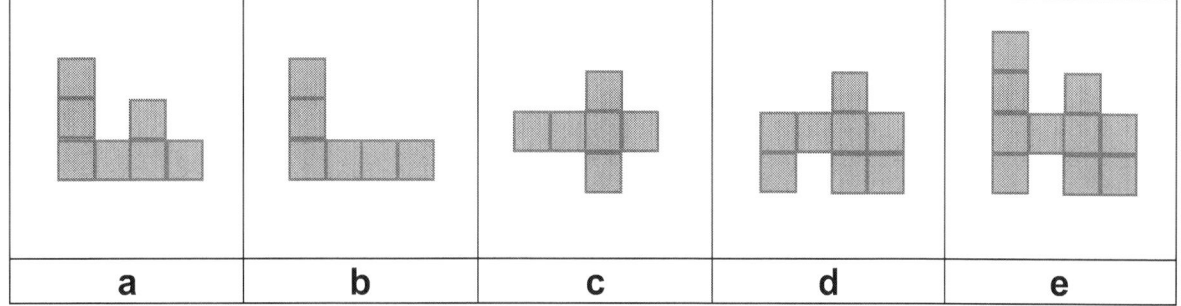

| a | b | c | d | e |

Question 6.4

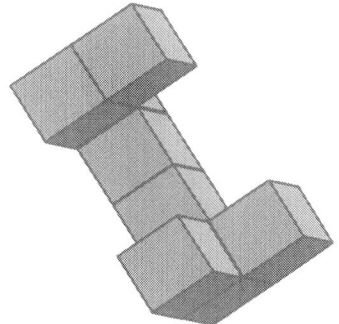

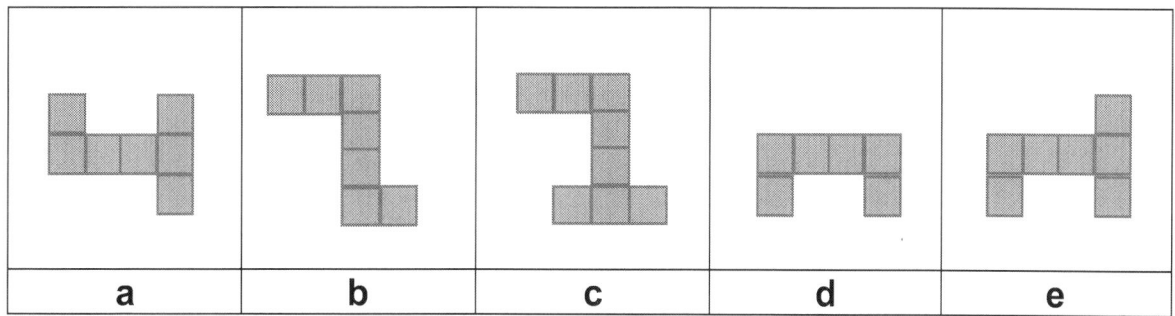

| a | b | c | d | e |

Question 6.5

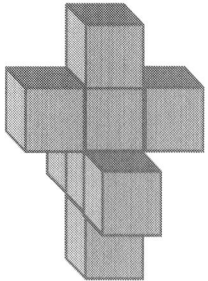

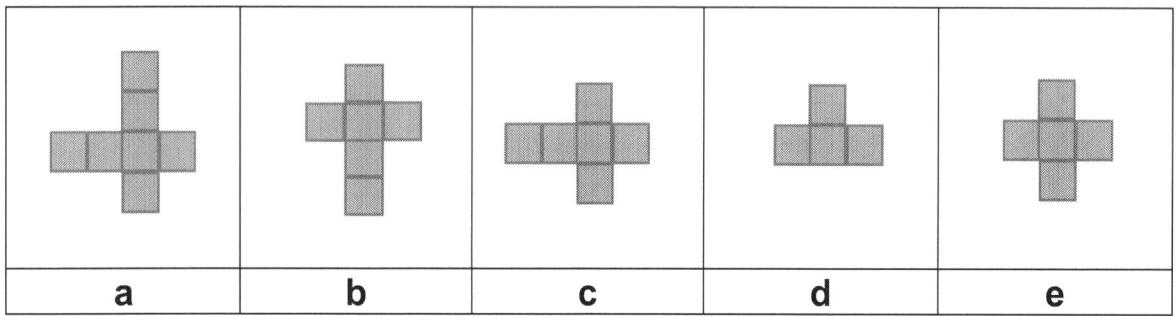

a	b	c	d	e

Question 6.6

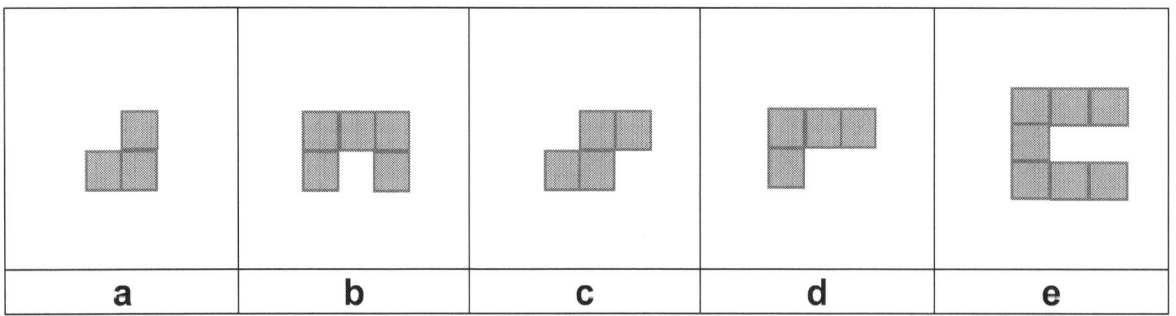

a	b	c	d	e

Question 6.7

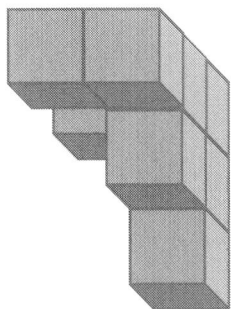

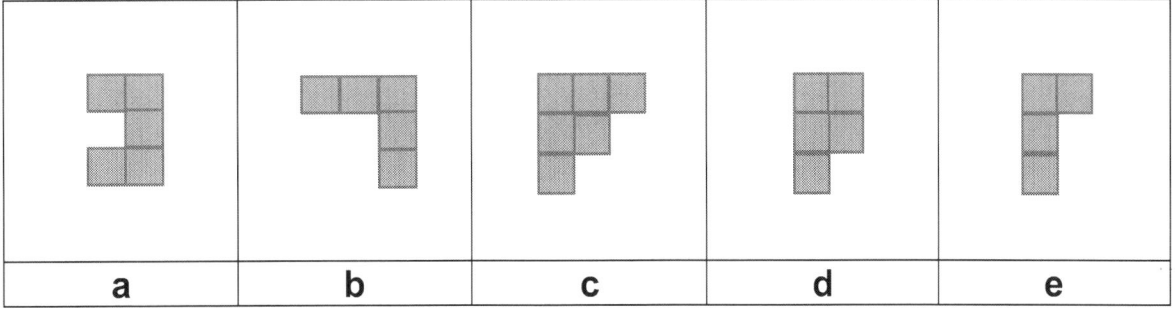

Question 6.8

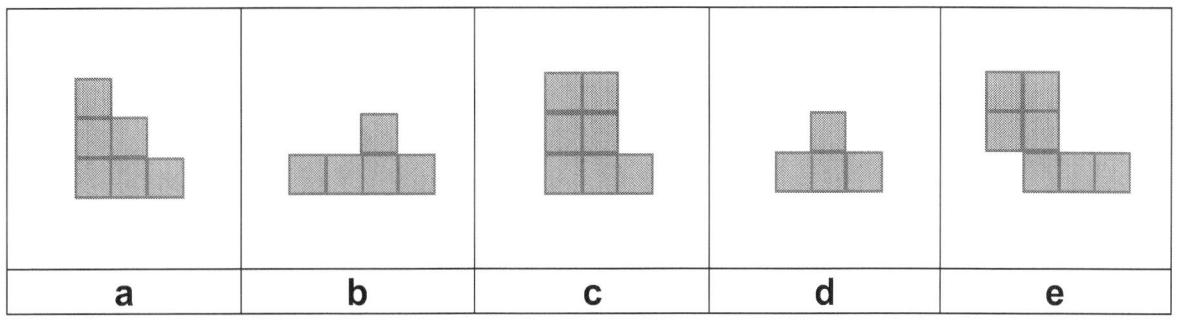

Question 6.9

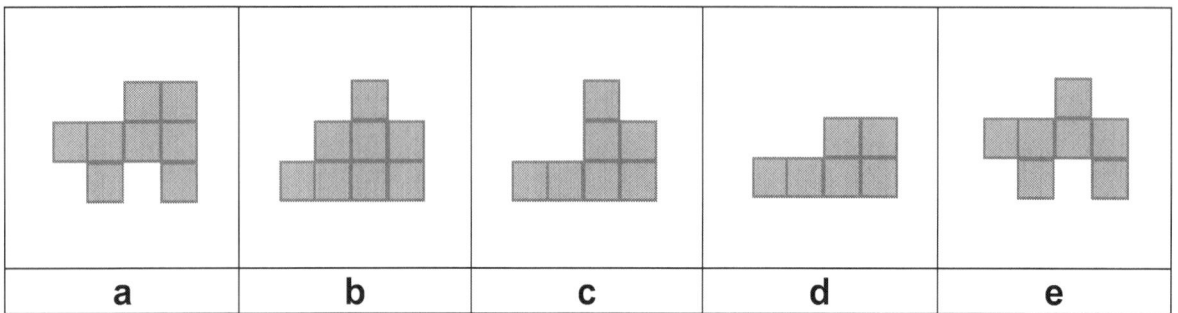

Question 6.10

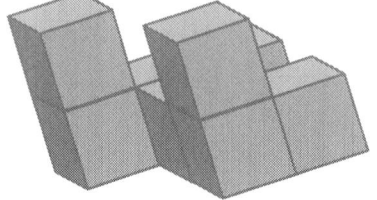

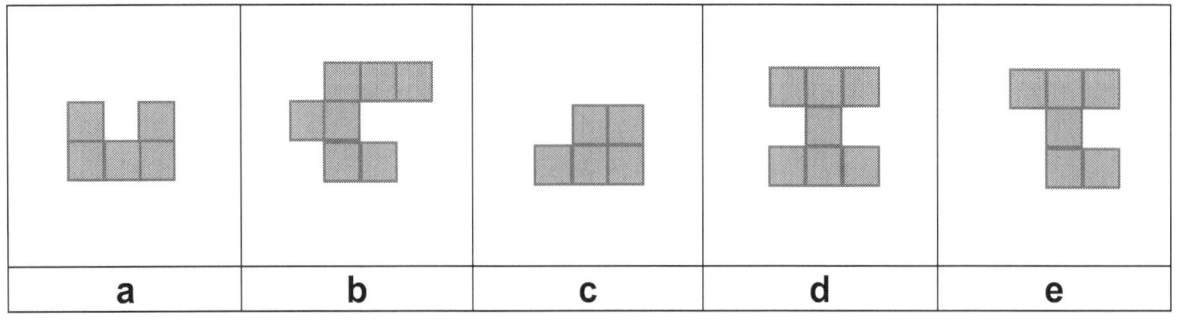

Question 6.11

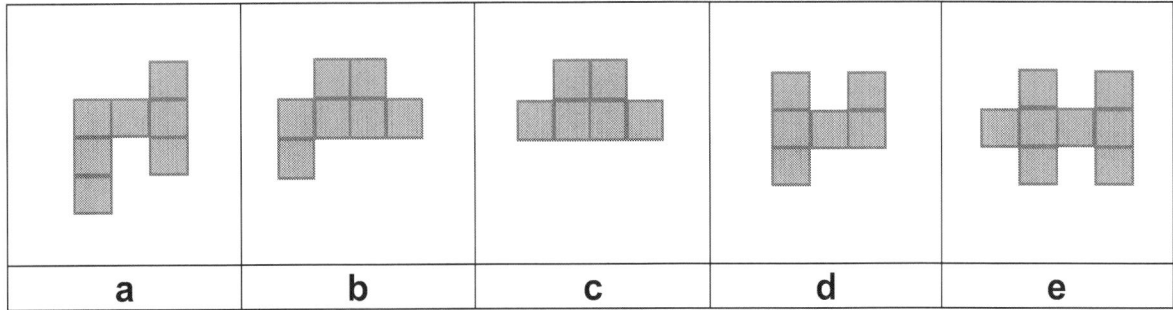

a	b	c	d	e

Question 6.12

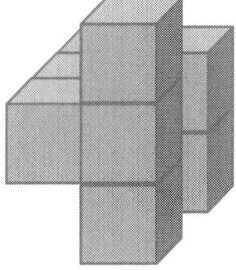

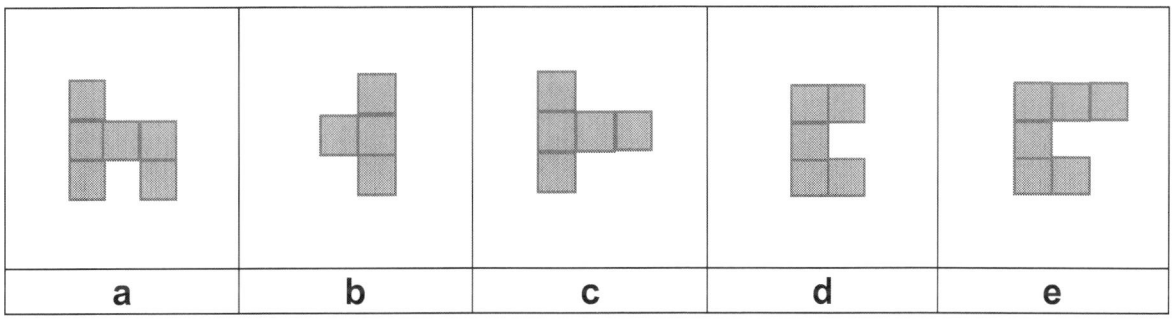

a	b	c	d	e

Type 6 Answers

6.1	D
6.2	E
6.3	B
6.4	D
6.5	E
6.6	B
6.7	A
6.8	E
6.9	D
6.10	E
6.11	A
6.12	D

Printed in Great Britain
by Amazon